Life at the Intersection

6

$$\frac{Q+14}{15}\ \ 16 \qquad 3^2$$

NW 18   16
25

Dec 5

Sep. 14 ③ hrs

Oct 14 ⑯
15

Nw. 18 ⑧

Dec 5 ③

㊷

(12 hr) × 4

3 hr ea

Life at the Intersection

Community, Class and Schooling

Carl E. James

Fernwood Publishing
Halifax and Winnipeg

Editing: Elizabeth Phinney
Cover design: John van der Woude
Printed and bound in Canada by Hignell Book Printing

Published in Canada by Fernwood Publishing
32 Oceanvista Lane
Black Point, Nova Scotia, B0J 1B0
and 748 Broadway Avenue, Winnipeg, Manitoba, R3G 0X3
www.fernwoodpublishing.ca

Fernwood Publishing Company Limited gratefully acknowledges the financial support
of the Government of Canada through the Canada Book Fund and the Canada Council
for the Arts, the Nova Scotia Department of Communities, Culture and Heritage,
the Manitoba Department of Culture, Heritage and Tourism under the Manitoba Publishers
Marketing Assistance Program and the Province of Manitoba, through the
Book Publishing Tax Credit, for our publishing program.

Library and Archives Canada Cataloguing in Publication

James, Carl, [date]
Life at the intersection: community, class and schooling / Carl E. James.

Includes bibliographical references.
ISBN 978-1-55266-470-4

1. Youth with social disabilities--Education--Ontario--Jane-Finch
(Toronto). 2. Youth--Ontario--Jane-Finch (Toronto)--Social conditions.
3. Jane-Finch (Toronto, Ont.)--Social conditions. I. Title.

LC4094.3.T6J34 2012   371.826'9409713541   C2011-908394-9

Contents

Acknowledgements

After many years of wanting to write, planning to write and working on "a book" about the community, it was a relief and very heartening to have received the email from editor Elizabeth Phinney that read: "Thanks so much for answering all of my queries, Carl. I do believe we are finished! Onward to production." Yes, this book has been a long time in coming and I have to thank the many people who, over the years, have encouraged me and contributed to my thinking through what I wanted to say, what I should say and what needed to be said, if indeed, this work is to be a counter narrative of the community and advance its social welfare.

I wish to start by acknowledging the many community members and workers with whom I spoke and who encouraged me in the process of writing. I am especially indebted to Kulsoom Anwer, who helped me to get started on this project, assisted with the writing of Chapter 2 and later provided her own reflections in the concluding chapter. Like Kulsoom, a number of community members acted as informal resources. I have recognized them in the Preface, but here, I wish to mention Trumaine Jackson and Sam Tecle, who shared their perspectives of growing up as young Black men in the community. In the late stage of the writing, Sam was one of my "go to" persons who answered my questions, provided clarification where needed and offered feedback on my ideas, assumptions and interpretation of things. Sam has also written his reflections, which appear in the concluding chapter. I owe a great deal of gratitude to Devon Jones, a committed teacher and youth worker with an infectious enthusiasm for change in the community, whose generous support and insights contributed to this work.

I am also grateful to the many teacher candidates in the "Urban Education" (ED/UR ED 3300) classes I co-taught at York University over the years with Stan Isoki, Pat Saul, Jackie Robinson and Kimberly Tavares-Carter and to the members of the graduate class (2010/11) in "Theory and Research in Language, Culture and Teaching" (ED5120) I co-taught with initiator, Professor Don Dippo. The exchanges in these classes comprised of community and non-community members not only stimulated my curiosity and gave insights into issues but also enriched this work. Thanks to my teaching colleagues for indulging me with my interest.

Over the past three years (2008–2011), the School and Community Engaged Education (SCEE) project, through which we worked with students, teachers and community members in the neighbourhood schools contributed immensely to this work. While this book does not report on findings from this invaluable Toronto District School Board/Faculty of Education partnership project, my experience in this project was beneficial. Therefore, to the SCEE program and research teams and participants, I express my sincere gratitude.

It was my long time friends, Alexander Francis, a youth worker in the community in the 1980s, and Clive Banton, a university contemporary and resident who, on separate occasions, gave me my first guided educational tour of the community. I hope that they approve of the use I have made of that early education. My thanks also to Alex (Frano, as we call him) for sharing his archival materials with me and answering my questions while I was writing the manuscript.

There is nothing like having reliable individuals willing to provide assistance when they receive a call from a far-away friend. Professor Howard Ramos, Dr. Jean Walrond-Patterson and Liza Lorenzetti were three such friends. They not only pointed me to sources of information, but also provided verifications and insights that I would not have been able to obtain otherwise. I am especially grateful to Howard — a consistent friend whom I have long been able to count on — for his support with data and helpful comments on parts of the manuscripts.

Sincere thanks to the many research assistants, Desmond Miller, Krsyta Pandolfi, Kulsoom Anwer, Sam Tecle, Adrian Worrell, Selom Chapman-Nyaho, Kai James and Tana Turner, who helped me at different stages and with the various versions of the manuscript — and special thank you to Desmond for his dependable help with the anchor leg to the finish. I very much appreciate the assistance of Kulsoom and Adrian with Chapters 2 and 5 respectively. Also to the many others who provided assistance to this project, researcher Dr. Rob Brown, former principal Barbara Taylor, youth worker and Vanier scholar Dani Kwan-Lafond and trustee Stephnie Payne for sharing their expertise, knowledge and reading of the issues in the community.

I acknowledge the support of colleagues Patricia Gagliardi-Ursua, Louise Gormley and Tara Fernandez at the Centre for Education and Community, others in the Faculty of Education and friends, including Patricia Hayes, Pat Saul, Sandra Schecter and Mary Anne Chambers, who supported me in the writing by providing information, needed assistance, commenting on my ideas or simply being present in the daily activities of living. In all these things Selom Chapman-Nyaho was a constant and I remain forever thankful to him. I also acknowledge with gratitude the small faculty grant I received for research assistance.

I started by mentioning Elizabeth Phinney's last email to me. That was an important email for it signalled that the huge task of editing, which she so ably performed, was now completed. I am sincerely grateful to her for her patience, detailed and careful revisions, and helpful suggestions, which have certainly strengthened the manuscript. And to cover designer, John van der Woude, thanks for the eloquent and creative representation of the story I am trying to tell. As always, the staff of Fernwood, Candida Hadley, Beverley Rach and Errol Sharpe were very accommodating. I remain truly grateful to them for their interest, support and confidence in this project, which were undoubtedly essential to competing this project.

Of course, family often indirectly and sometimes directly plays considerable roles in every project. In this regard, Kai, Dorne and Sammy Milderine deserve my deep appreciation for the ways they supported and indulged me in my work.

Preface

It is fair to say that every major city has an area or neighbourhood that is stereotyped as "tough," or, in media terms, "troubled." These neighbourhoods are typically characterized by low-income housing, poverty and a high proportion of racial and/or ethnic minority members. And in immigrant-receiving metropolitan cities, these neighbourhoods tend to become "reception areas" for new arrivals. The dwellings in these neighbourhoods are mostly low-rise and highrise apartment buildings and some townhouses. Taken altogether, these neighbourhoods often earn the distinction of being the city's most densely populated and culturally diverse areas, where residents have limited green space and recreational facilities. Living in such "close" quarters with limited alternatives, outlets or means (social and economic) to get away, there should be little wonder that interactions among residents could result in tensions and conflict that, after a while, could escalate into violence.

It is true that growing up in such a neighbourhood need not be detrimental to a healthy social, emotional and cultural existence. There are, no doubt, advantages. Young people could grow to appreciate cultural diversity, having interacted with people of different racial, ethnic and language backgrounds — a vital experience in our multicultural society. And having worked hard in school, they will appreciate their academic success (e.g., a university education) that enables them to work at a "good" job with compensation that places them in a position to leave the community. Of course, we teach young people that our society makes this kind of social mobility possible for them; specifically, that equality of opportunity, meritocracy and democracy exist in our society, and individuals should not limit themselves to the circumstances into which they were born. Nor should they think themselves trapped in the community in which they are growing up. Schools play a key role in bringing this message to young people with the expectation that, inequities notwithstanding, students will learn that it is up to them to work hard, hold high aspirations, apply themselves to their studies and be optimistic about their possibilities in life — an expectation that is difficult for some youth to realize

But what happens when the community is branded one of the most "troubled" in the country? How can schooling help prepare students for life inside and outside of the community? What should educators be doing in order to nurture students' ambitions and optimism that comes with confidence in their sense of agency? I come to these questions after many years of observation and work in the community with students, teachers and community workers. And while I had some answers to these questions from the research I had undertaken since 1994, I remained justifiably interested in writing a book in which I would explore more thoroughly what it means (or takes) to grow up, go to school and think of (or plan) a future while residing in Jane and Finch. But there were two questions that I felt I needed to answer before undertaking such a project.

My first question was: Am I the person to write this book? If so, with whom, given my "outsider" status? As an educator who engages in activist research that gives attention to the privileges embedded in the unequal relationship between researcher and researched, or between myself as a university teacher and community members, I take seriously the expectation that what I do (the research or writing) comes from having established a trustworthy, respectful and ethical relationship with members of the community. Furthermore, I fully understand that whatever I produce needs to be meaningful and useful to the community in their resistance to their branding, their struggles to establish themselves as a decent community and their hope for their young people and the community as a whole. To this end, I sought the advice and assistance of a number of people who either lived or worked, or who had done so in the past, in the community. In fact, this project was started about four years earlier with Kulsoom Anwer, a former resident of the community and a former student in the Urban Education class I taught at York University. Kulsoom had to drop out for family reasons. Nevertheless, she continued to comment on the writing, and her contributions can be seen in the community profile (Chapter 2) and in the Conclusion. Others, such as Samuel Tecle, Pat Saul, Charis Newton-Thompson, Elise Davidson, Troy Fraser, Devon Jones and Joesiann Nelson, assisted by reading drafts of the chapters, filling in missing information, providing insights and analytical points, and commenting on the efficacy of what I had written (including the appropriateness of the book title). In short, these people became, in research parlance, "editorial advisors" and "critical friends."

My second question was: In publishing such a book, should I name the community or give it a pseudonym — a common "ethical" practice in research? I admit to having discussions on this question with colleagues at the university who have published works on these troubled areas. Many of them agree that naming the community is useful, for there is a need to provide counter-narratives of specific areas that challenge what is often put out by the media. With this understanding (more likely apprehension), I put the question to my critical friends and advisors, as well as to a graduate class I was co-teaching with Professor Don Dippo at Yorkgate

Mall in the York University–TD Community Engagement Centre, located at Jane and Finch. The course was "Practitioner Research," where we explored the responsibilities, ethics and challenges in conducting community research. The twenty participants were mostly teachers, school administrators, and social service and health care workers. Approximately half of the participants either currently work in, or are former residents of, the community. In the class in which we talked about research ethics and process, I shared that I was in process of writing this book and wanted their thoughts on whether I should name the community or use a pseudonym. I was particularly looking for a response from the class members who worked and lived in Jane and Finch, since they brought important knowledge and insights from the community (though informed by their particular lived experiences). The response was that I should name the community, because they expected that I would write against media representation and the exclusionary practices of marginalization, racialization, criminalization and others that serve to stigmatize, oppress and silence them. I promised that I would try to do that and went on to ask if what they expected would not be best written by someone who lived in the community. The unanimous response was "not necessarily," for as one community worker and former resident said, "Some people in the community are just as likely to damage the community, make it look bad with what they write. Insiders could be worse, for outside people might assume that insiders have a vested interest in the community and represent a more authentic view of the community. But in actuality they may perpetuate the negative stereotypes and images of the community with what they write. This could serve to validate the views that outsiders hold of the community." Indeed, it is usually difficult to accept the views of superficial, uncritical observers. Nonetheless, there is something instructive, even helpful, in hearing or reading what an individual has to say — notwithstanding knowing our respective biases or prejudices. I concede, however, that there are limits to encouraging publications or utterances that do not inspire or sustain hope, especially when what is said does not take into account structural or systemic factors. But then again, how do you engage or challenge an idea unless it is articulated?

While I am not an insider to the community, I do not consider myself an outsider either. For while I have not lived in Jane and Finch, I have long years of working in and/or with colleagues and friends from the community. Hence, I believe that I bring to this project a useful amount of familiarity, knowledge and insight. In fact, my experience with the community dates back to the early 1980s when I worked part-time at Central Neighbourhood House (CNH) as a youth worker with youth from Regent Park, a public housing community (two blocks east of the House) in downtown Toronto. The youth with whom I worked were from the Caribbean (most of them from Jamaica) and had recently come to Canada to join their parents (mostly mothers). I too had emigrated from the Caribbean and, at that time, had been living in Canada for about ten years. It was through the friends of the youth who attended our weekend (Friday night and Saturday) programs that I learned about Jane and Finch.

My other early connection to the community came through the Maroons Community Organization, which held youth programs at the newly built Driftwood Community Centre. The program attracted hundreds of Black youth, many of them recent immigrants from the Caribbean, with profiles, needs and issues similar to the youth with whom I was working in downtown Toronto. The youth and their parents needed educational support that would assist them in their adjustment to the Ontario education system, as well as space for social, cultural and recreational activities. The Maroons organization, run by Alexander Francis, had programs geared to addressing these needs, but the organization was most famous for its annual basketball tournament at Tate McKenzie recreation centre at York University. The tournament drew teams from as far away as Montreal, Halifax and the United States.

I attended a number of these basketball tournaments with the senior basketball team from CNH, coached by my co-worker Denny Hunte. Hundreds of youth participated in Maroon's Thursday evening and Sunday afternoon program activities, to the extent that, as Francis noted, they sometimes had to close the doors of the Centre to comply with fire regulations. This large attendance, or as Francis put it, "gathering of hundreds of Black youth in one place," was of such concern to the Centre's administrator as well as community members that a meeting was called at the nearby school to discuss "what to do with nigger night," as Francis recalls. Nevertheless, the program continued for about nine years.

In the late 1980s I worked with the Jane and Finch Concerned Citizens Association to develop a proposal (ASPIRE) for the North York Board of Education that was designed to address the educational needs of the youth in the area schools. For a number of years, the organization had been in conversations with the Board about the poor educational performance of students, their disengagement, their high drop-out rates and the lack of parental involvement in the schools. The program was never implemented. However, when I joined the Faculty of Education at York University in the early 1990s, a year after the faculty had implemented the Westview Partnership — a partnership between the faculty and the Board of Education — I became a member of the Partnership program, conceived as an "Urban Education" program. A Steering Committee made up of faculty, school, and university administrators and community members directed the program of research and other related activities. I participated in the outreach, and was faculty liaison with the co-ordinating mentor teachers who supervised the teacher candidates placed in the high schools. As faculty liaison, I periodically visited the school and facilitated workshops there with the teacher candidates and their mentor teachers. We explored topics specific to the teaching experiences of the teacher candidates, the teachers, students and parents. These included issues related to adolescent life and development, immigrant parents and children, educational aspiration and teaching in culturally diverse classrooms.

By the mid-1990s, the faculty introduced the "Urban Education" course, which brought together all the teacher candidates from all levels of schooling. This course that I developed and first taught was intended to examine issues related to schooling in urban settings characterized by low socio-economic conditions, high population density and diversity related to ethnic, racial, religious, migration and cultural difference. The class was co-taught with a teacher from a high school, and interested teachers, parents and community members were invited to participate — although very few did. The course was first taught in a middle school in the area, but after about three years, it was moved to the university. It was in one of these classes that I first encountered Shakti (pseudonym), who stood out in class because of where she sat with her seven friends (mostly students of colour) and who would challenge her classmates to think differently of Jane and Finch — a community she claimed to know more about than any other student in the room. The table at which Shakti and her friends sat was referred to as "the centre table" — so named because of its location in the middle of the classroom. While I shared their interest in changing these future teachers' understanding and accepted narrative of Jane and Finch, and more generally of working-class people, I was concerned about their strategy, which served to intimidate and silence their peers. My colleague and co-course director, Pat Saul, and I came under heavy criticism from the "centre table" because we were viewed as being "too soft" on the teacher candidates.

Despite the challenges, over the past three years, I, along with others, have been working in four schools in the area on an inclusive education project, School and Community Education and Community, in partnership with the Toronto District School Board. The project is intended to help teachers develop and work with curriculum that is related to the particular experiences, needs, interests and aspirations of the students and parents. The project team that I led, which includes faculty members, teachers and graduate students, see inclusive curriculum as one that takes into account the local community in which students and parents live, learn and play. Hence, teachers must necessarily have a good knowledge of the community, something that they can gain through (among other channels) listening to their students, talking with parents (outside of parent-teacher visits and calling about a student), walking through the community, going to the malls, shopping in the area and familiarizing themselves (in part through visits) with the services or programs of the community agencies. I believe that the school program and curriculum that are rooted in the experiences of students, which recognize the social and cultural capital or "community cultural wealth" (Yosso 2005) of the students, their parents and community, will serve to engage them in their learning and therefore reverse their underperformance, low educational achievement and high push/drop-out rates.

In this book, I look beyond the intersection, and in concert with the residents of the Jane and Finch community who continuously struggle to change its existing narrative, I provide a counter-narrative that hopefully will contribute to social and educational change. I leave the bigger discussion about the lives of the people generally for another book, another time and other authors, and concentrate here on the schooling lives and experiences of young people who are growing up or have grown up in the Jane-Finch community.

Of course, this book is by no means the end of the conversation I wish to have about the community or such communities in general; consider it an addition to the many conversations that I have had so far. This is my attempt to share experiences, learnings, and new and different perspectives of the community. And instead of being "too soft" — heeding Shakti's advice — I hope that I have been able to engage critically with the issues under discussion, showing the role of structures and individuals' agency in attending to the complex and shifting problems that are inherent in these communities. All things considered, I hope that instead of silencing conversation, the book opens it up, along with raising questions — even instigating them.

Chapter 1

Community, Stigmatization and Opportunities

Where are you from? Where do you live? What school did you attend? Through these frequently asked questions we often try to learn about each other, particularly in our attempt to "place" someone within a social, economic, cultural or geographic context of a city or society generally. For some people, the answers to these questions are a source of pride, and as such, they respond with little thought. For others, however, experience has taught them to avoid answering these questions because of the stigma and stereotypes that are attached to their community. This resistance to stereotyping is understandable, since where we live is more than a geographic space. It is part of our identity, and it informs the way we think about ourselves in national, racial, ethnic, social and economic terms. Our identities are as much products of our communities as the society in which we live, and we are shaped or socialized by the institutions — familial, educational, religious, social, recreational, cultural and legal (or justice) — with which we interact in the process of becoming respectful, participating citizens of the society. Indeed, the complex interlocking relationships between the micro and macro — between the self, the community or neighbourhood, and larger society — are inescapable. Therefore, the notion that individuals are autonomous beings created by circumstances of their own making, who hold their fate within their own hands, is misleading. The fact is, we are all products of the communities or neighbourhoods in which we live and grew up, and people judge us by what they know — or think they know — about them.

Take, for instance, what has been said of residents of the Jane and Finch neighbourhood. A colleague, Ms. Brown (pseudonym), recalled talking to a group of dinner party guests in August 2010 about a summer government program she led and had helped to initiate to assist youth in neighbourhoods that are often stigmatized by negative stereotypes. In response to the stereotyping, Ms. Brown had heard from the youth that they must use the addresses of friends or relatives who live in other neighbourhoods "if they were to have any hope of receiving responses to their job applications." The youth program had identified this neighbourhood as one of many with lower-than-average income levels and school graduation rates, and higher-than-average unemployment and crime rates. Obviously sceptical about the value of such targeted programs, one guest commented that "when a youth from the Jane and Finch neighbourhood screws up and has to be fired, who could fault the employer for not hiring any more youth from that community?" Ms. Brown responded, "If that youth were from Thornhill [a middle-class suburban community north of Toronto], no one would dream of suggesting that the employer should not hire any more youth from Thornhill."

Generalizations like that above about people within the Jane-Finch community contribute to the social, educational and economic conditions faced by residents. While it is understandable to have expectations of members of a certain community — given that collectively each of us bears some responsibility for whatever goes on within our respective communities — the above example illustrates how expectations are differentially applied to people living in particular communities. Such generalizations and expectations also have to do with the stigmatization of Jane and Finch as a perpetually "troubled" community. The media help to construct and sustain this branding, often because of the crime, violence and social conditions (Hall 2008), which scholars have long demonstrated are often by-products of low-income, high-density neighbourhoods (Hidalgo 1997; López 2002).

Wacquant (2008: 1) writes that "stigmatized neighbourhoods [are] situated at the very bottom of the hierarchical system of places that comprise the metropolis." These are areas, he says, where social problems fester and where "urban outcasts" reside, resulting in such areas getting "disproportionately negative attention from the media, politicians and stare managers." Wacquant goes on to say that stigmatized neighbourhoods become known

> to outsiders and insiders alike, as the "lawless zones," the "problem estates," the "no-go areas" or the "wild districts" of the city, territories of deprivation and dereliction to be feared, fled from and shunned because they are — or such is their reputation, but in these matters perception contributes powerfully to fascinating reality — hotbeds of violence, vice and social dissolution. Owing to the halo of danger and dread that enshrouds them and to the scorn that afflicts their inhabitants, a variegated mix of dispossessed households, dishonoured minorities and disenfranchised immigrants, they are typically depicted from above and from afar in sombre and monochrome tones. And social life in them appears to be somewhat the same: barren, chaotic and brutish. (1)

In this context, the situation in which residents of "troubled" communities find themselves is not only a product of their own aspirations, expectations and behaviours, but also that of, and often more so, the prevailing attitudes, perceptions and beliefs found among members of the society (take, for example, the scepticism of the party guest, above). All of this is related to the unequal socio-economic system of power, privilege and opportunity. That is why the daily lives and social outcomes of the residents of these stigmatized communities are much more affected by economic recessions when the cost of living increases; or when neighbourhood schools close and children must walk a considerable distance to school or commute (which adds more cost to schooling); or when governments charge fees for social services and recreational programs; or when developers move in to gentrify the area and in the process displace residents who are unable to afford the new high cost of living in the neighbourhood.

Many of us, including educators, are often woefully oblivious to some of the stark truths about society's role in creating "troubled" communities and the consequent "at-risk" students from these communities. Clearly, communities "are not islands apart from the rest of society, rather, members are very much a part of that society, including its injustices" (Henze 2005: 257), and by extension, its injuries. Rather than seeing the "trouble" within the community and the "at-risk" situation of the youth as self-generated (blame-the-victim ethos), we need to place emphasis on the structures that create and perpetuate the conditions that make them so. However, the notion of personal responsibility — sustained by the rugged individualism embedded in Western culture — is far too powerful and alluring to suspend or let go of, for it enables us to maintain the appealing "Canadian/American Dream." To suggest that our life circumstances, the neighbourhoods in which we live, the schools we attend and the opportunities we are able to access are as much determined by our individual efforts as structural factors mediated by characteristics such as class, race, gender and citizenship is to destroy a dearly held belief system that governs the way we think of ourselves, our communities and our capacity to influence and control what happens to us.

Nevertheless, despite the structures that present barriers to their social, educational and occupational participation and attainment in society, members of "troubled" communities do exercise agency, or at least try to, in their bid to counter the negativity that afflicts and blights their community. In this regard, they use the labelling of themselves as troublemakers, social misfits, educationally limited and welfare recipients to inspire them to hold high aspirations, and to participate in society in ways that would ensure their own social, educational and economic success if only meritocracy and democracy governed the actions of decision-makers (James 2009). Furthermore, understanding how much their hopes and opportunities are entangled in the profile of their community, members will take steps to challenge these stereotypes whenever they can. This practice was made clear in a recent meeting of residents of the Jane-Finch community in Toronto. The meeting was called by researchers who wanted input from community residents. After hearing from the investigators and other members of the research team, one community member, seemingly fearful or ambivalent, and concerned that the researchers might use their research to re-inscribe the prevailing narrative of their community as "troubled," came up to the microphone and started by saying, "We are more than an intersection..." — a reference to how the community is named. But more importantly, he was saying that beyond the intersection is a community of hardworking people who aspire to live productive lives as educated and industrious citizens — a reality that many residents of that community believe is not often recognized by members of the larger Toronto and Canadian society.

This examination of what exists beyond the intersection of these two major streets, Jane and Finch, is particularly significant when we take into account what the dinner guest (referred to above) said to Ms. Brown. And in a recent discussion with some visiting German teachers who came to Toronto to learn more about, and observe, Canadian multiculturalism at work, one participant indicated that one of the areas that her suburban Toronto host warned her against visiting was Jane and Finch. Jane and Finch is known nationally as one of Canada's most "troubled" neighbourhoods. When disaffected racialized youth rioted in Paris in the autumn of 2005, demanding social and economic justice, Jane and Finch is where Canadian reporters looked when they asked: "Can it happen here?"[1] The reporters' and citizens' gaze was also likely inspired by the number of murders in Toronto that year, termed "the year of the gun." The fifty-plus gun-related murders of that year — many of them young Black men shot by their Black peers — involved few gunmen and murder victims from Jane and Finch. Yet even though many of the incidents took place outside of that community, Jane and Finch became a community of much concern.[2] It was this intersection to which then Prime Minister Paul Martin went to announce his government's plan of action to address the social problems precipitating the violence that was affecting all of Toronto. It was also to this community that CBC radio host Shelagh Rogers went for "a walk" to find out "what was really going on" (Weins 2005).

In a profile of the national under-sixteen soccer team, Saskatoon's *Star Phoenix* described one young team member, Jerome Baker, as coming from "the Toronto slum known as Jane and Finch."[3] The article told of how soccer saved Baker, and in doing so, made him an exception to the rule. The idea put forth was that it is possible to do well even though you come from a "slum" environment. While such positive news stories might be seen as the media's attempt to provide "balanced" coverage of area residents, they can also be quite unflattering in that they carry an implicit message that suggests others in the community are not similarly working to achieve better lives.

Jane and Finch became even more infamous in May 2007 when Jordan Manners, a fifteen-year-old student, was shot and killed in his local high school. The media dubbed this incident as the first instance of a student being murdered in a Canadian school, even though in 1999 two students had been killed in a school shooting in Taber, Alberta. The difference between the Taber and Toronto shootings is, of course, context. The Tabor high school is in a small, mostly White town, where such an incident is supposedly highly unusual. Students at the Toronto "urban" high school were considered to be "at risk" because of the "troubled" community where they lived and where such incidents tend to be seen as an inevitability — something just "waiting to happen." The notion of urban and "urban school students" conjures up images of slums or ghettos found in American cities. These neighbourhoods are thought to be populated mostly by African Americans. And while African Canadians might not be the largest ethno-racial group at Jane and Finch, there is a tendency to categorize it as a "Black" area. This is likely why, as noted above, Torontonians, the media and government representatives were looking at Jane and Finch during "the year of the gun."

In their analysis of local media reports following Jordan Manners' death, O'Grady, Parnaby and Schikschneit (2010: 66) write that the media's framing of the "death was very much in keeping with the idea that the community at Jane and Finch represents an urban underclass, with a high concentration of welfare-dependent, visible-minority, single-parent households residing in subsidized housing" (see also Hall 2008). According to the authors, this growing "culturally distinct" population of working class people — different from the "traditional" working class, and having "little resemblance to 'us'" — are people about whom dominant members of many Western societies have been concerned, for they represent the "alien other" whose values and morals are inconsistent with the dominant family values, education and work ethic, individual enterprise and lawfulness.

Canada's "Troubled" Communities

Jane and Finch is home to about eighty thousand people of diverse ethnic, racial and religious backgrounds, most of whom are second-plus-generation Canadians. Among the ethnic heritages represented are Italians, South Asians (mostly Indians and Sri Lankans), Asians (mostly Vietnamese and Cambodians), Africans (mostly Somalis and Ghanians) and Caribbeans (particularly African Caribbeans). Located in the northwestern section of

Toronto, part of the community contains high-density highrise apartment buildings and townhouses that were built in the 1960s as social housing for the increasing numbers of immigrants and refugees arriving at the time — a need that the buildings continue to fill. The area also contains condominiums (owned and rented) and single-family homes. Given its location in relation to the downtown core, the area would have been considered an inner (or in-between) suburb of Toronto — a suburban area within the boundaries of the City of Toronto. However, given the characteristics of the community, the area is referred to as an "urban area" or "inner city," and the schools are referred to as "urban schools," with "urban" being a handy euphemism for so much that is racialized these days.

Essentially, Jane and Finch has become a national reference or part of the Canadian lexicon representing the quintessential "troubled" and "at-risk" community (see Hall, 2008; Richardson, 2008). But issues that contribute to the categorization of Jane and Finch as a "troubled" community are certainly not unique to this area. Indeed, there are other communities in Toronto and Canada with similar issues. So why has Jane and Finch become the archetype of a troubled community? A look at some of the other stigmatized neighbourhoods in Canada might point to some answers.

Vancouver's Downtown Eastside, often referred to as "skid row," is generally regarded as Canada's poorest urban postal code. The neighbourhood of about sixteen thousand residents is made up of people who are homeless; in transition to homes in other locations, and few, if any, families with children and community activists. In recent years, there has been an increase in the diversity of the population, many of them immigrants and refugees, particularly Asians, and Aboriginals in disproportionate numbers. Known for its high incidence of poverty, drug use, crime, HIV/ Aids, hepatitis infection and exploitative sex trade, any involvement with the Downtown Eastside is seen as synonymous with unavoidable danger. Compared to the media depiction of Jane and Finch as a racialized enclave from which an individual is expected to, and can, move up and away from, Vancouver's Downtown Eastside tends to be perceived as a neighbourhood with people who are trapped because of their poor individual choices and lack of "morality." As Stefan Christoff and Sawsan Kalache (2007: 42) state in their article "The Poorest Postal Code," the "Downtown Eastside remains a consistent reminder of the social and human realities of urban poverty."

Once a small town, the community of Forest Lawn, which celebrated its 100th anniversary in 2010, is considered to be Calgary's "best example of intercultural richness and co-existence" (Elise [pseudonym], Personal communication, February 2011) as well as one where poverty, stigmatization, violence and crime differentiate the lives of its residents.

The population of 7,676 (City of Calgary 2010) includes Aboriginals, Asians (particularly Filipino, Pakistani, Chinese), South Asians, Africans (particularly Sudanese) and Europeans. Uniquely designated as Greater Forest Lawn because of the number of neighbourhoods that make up the community, the main thoroughfare, International Avenue (or 17th Ave. SE), is recognized as the hub for shopping, restaurants and services — a number of them operated by Vietnamese and Middle Eastern people. With a poverty rate higher than the city's average and a greater number of sole-parent households (Statistics Canada 2006), the communities of Greater Forest Lawn suffer from the resultant labelling and stigmatization by other Calgarians. Crime and safety are said to be ongoing concerns — something that area residents and workers (including police) are working collaboratively to change. As one community worker stated (Elise [pseudonym], Personal communication, February 2011):

> The image and stigma of Forest Lawn as a dangerous community cannot be viewed without a critical race and class analysis.... There are families that work in low-paid and highly exploitative jobs just to see their children turn to crime or gangs. It is important to acknowledge and particularly respond to the power/oppression issues behind people's circumstances. On a personal note, I am a sort of second "mother" (that is what they call me) to two youth from one of these neighbourhoods who are part of that story. I'm really hoping that they make it through.

The community of Alberta Avenue, with a population of about 6,900, is one of Edmonton, Alberta's, oldest neighbourhoods, predating World War II. Once renowned for its historical significance, it is now seen as one of Edmonton's most blighted communities. It has moved from a community composed of predominantly Europeans, to one of Aboriginals, immigrants and refugees (for example, Somalians and Sudanese). In its report on how various communities compared with each other as places to live in Edmonton, the *Edmonton Journal* showed that, based on a number of social, familial, health, crime, education, income and other indicators, Alberta Avenue received the lowest scores (Ruttan 2007). The report showed that about one in four residents relied on the food bank, and well over five hundred households lived at or below the low-income level established by Statistics Canada. The rate of movement from the community was about twice that of other residential areas. This is understandable given the higher-than-average crime rates (mainly property crime and prostitution), the number of single-parent households and the special education needs of young people.

In 2008, Saskatoon was inaugurated by *MacLean's* magazine as one of the most dangerous cities in Canada (MacQueen 2008). While mostly sensationalized rhetoric, Saskatoon's West Side (which is commonly referred to as "alphabet city" because of street names such as Avenue A, B, C) is a community stigmatized by its growing level of poverty, racialized housing and a highly segregated population of predominantly Aboriginals. Similar to Jane and Finch, concerns about youth gangs and the mounting levels of drug trafficking and robberies in the community have contributed to significant levels of police surveillance or over-policing (sometimes unjustified). For a community that has historically remained more or less homogenous (with some of the lowest levels of immigration and racial minority population), the West Side is often used as a reference point for anything to do with social problems. Further, ongoing patterns of inequity and social exclusion and high levels of school attrition rates (J. Wood 2011) are often explained away by "cultural" differences and ongoing racist discourses regarding the presumed "ineptitude" of the Aboriginal population.

Similar in character to Saskatoon's racially segregated urban area, Winnipeg's North End neighbourhood, located to the north and northwest of downtown Winnipeg, is regarded as that city's "troubled" community. In 2006, the Aboriginal population in Winnipeg was over 10 percent, and while the North End is ethnically diverse, the Aboriginal population has remained fairly stable within this inner-city neighbourhood. As such, the Aboriginal population is over-represented in programs that attempt to address addiction, homelessness and gang affiliation. DeVerteuil and Wilson (2010: 501), citing Peters and Hanselmann, opined that even with ongoing marginalization and racialization, as well as federal, provincial and municipal neglect, Winnipeg's North End has seen the establishment of Aboriginal-focused and self-governed social services. Yet, many people might argue that while culturally appropriate services are warranted, it "may also facilitate the containment and control of people that society generally deems disruptive and unproductive" (501).

Little Burgundy (or *la petite Bourgogne*) is located in the southwest borough of Montreal and was once the centre of the railway transportation and employment headquarters for the Canadian Pacific Railway. Beginning in the 1880s, African Americans were hired as temporary workers and served as porters and dining car attendants for the railway system. Since then, Little Burgundy has come to be seen as Montreal's Black community (which later came to include Caribbean immigrants and African Nova Scotians). The Oscar Peterson Park, located within the community, is viewed as being plagued by drug dealing and other criminal activities. However, since the 1980s, Little Burgundy has undergone various phases of gentrification. A similar and more recently identified "troubled" neighbourhood in Montreal is Saint-Michel. While one of the most ethnically diverse neighbourhoods in Quebec (i.e., home to Italians, Haitians, Asians, French Canadians, etc.), since the 1990s Saint-Michel has been deemed Montreal's most dangerous inner-city neighbourhood due to its persistent street gang problems, fuelled by negative press coverage. However, since the late 1990s, the presence of Cirque du Soleil's headquarters has fostered signs of urban renewal and interest.

Discussions about Halifax's "troubled" zones tend to focus on Uniacke Square and Spryfield. After bulldozing Africville in the 1960s, in the early 1970s the provincial government built public housing to accommodate its former residents on Gottingen Street, in an area known as Uniacke Square (still other residents were moved to Mulgrave Park, also in Halifax's North End). The housing was intended for the displaced Africville's Black residents, whose presence in Nova Scotia dates back to the American Revolution, the War of 1812 and the U.S. Civil War periods, when they came to Canada as refugees, slaves and freed slaves. Known as a community with a transient population, today the population of Uniacke Square is made up, not only of former Africville residents and their descendants, but other Canadians and immigrants (including Africans). Despite this diversity, the community continues to be perceived as a Black residential area with high levels of unemployment and social problems related in part to criminal activity. Jim Silver (2008: 2) argues that the issues facing "inner-city public housing" and gentrification "are placing Uniacke Square and its tenants at risk." Writing about a condo project planned for the area in the *Globe and Mail*, Chris Benjamin (2010) relates that the community of Spryfield, which has a slightly more diverse population, has issues that resemble those of Uniacke Square. In recent years, this community has been developing a reputation based on gang violence, drug dealing and related crimes.

Clearly, Jane and Finch is not the only "troubled" or "at-risk" community in Canada, yet it remains the most notorious in Canadians' consciousness and imagination. Why is this the case? What does Jane and Finch represent? And what internal and external factors contribute to the creation of these "at-risk" neighbourhoods and Jane and Finch in particular? What goes on in these communities is not, as many would like to believe, the product of flawed and limited people who just happen to share racialized and working-class backgrounds. Rather, it is the consequence of inequitable socio-economic structures that mediate individuals' social circumstances as well as their opportunities and possibilities. In the case of Jane and Finch, the fact that it is located in Canada's media headquarters and most populated city, is closely watched and scrutinized by law enforcement officers and is home to a significant number of racialized Canadians of immigrant background (the majority of whom are perceived to be Blacks) likely plays a significant role in its continued notoriety and image as a "troubled" community.

Media Discourses and the Racialization of Space

With a population of some 5.5 million people and as the country's major destination for immigrants, it is understandable that the Greater Toronto Area (GTA) would be Canada's largest English-based electronic and print media market. It is arguable, then, that media reports and editorials would more often report on and be slanted toward the issues, concerns and interests of Torontonians. In a media-saturated world, information about local, national and international events and issues is increasingly being communicated. The media play a major, if not a vital, role, not only in structuring popular or dominant discourses, but also in how individuals acquire information that subsequently influences and shapes their ideologies, beliefs and perceptions of reality. Contrary to the liberal mantra of the free and self-determining, information and the discourse in which it is couched is never impartial or objective but is structured by the institutional ethos from which it originates. As well, given how the media is market-driven, sensational or divisive, reporting often sells, and community members are often rendered powerless to combat unfair reporting.

Surely in Canada, as in Britain, according to van Dijk (2000), media reports are wrought with negative portrayals and special "code-words" relating to such things as the social and economic problems of immigrants and ethnic minorities ("Other Canadians"); their employment, housing and welfare situation; and their (cultural) "difference" and deviance, particularly in terms of their likelihood to engage in violence, crime, drugs and prostitution. What is troubling is how, through these portrayals, readers come to understand and associate particular issues with certain groups, especially, as van Dijk (2000: 37) points out, "white readers," who have "few daily experiences with minorities… have few alternative sources for information about minorities" and observe behaviours among minority members as a threat to national security. Insofar as Jane and Finch serves as a physical embodiment of a community with "problems" populated by Other Canadians, in the absence of media reports that present a different more hospitable image, the community will continue to suffer from deeply entrenched assumptions, ambivalences and resentments, and thereby always have "troubles."

Another factor that renders Jane and Finch as the national "trouble" zone is police surveillance. In tandem with biased reporting, which prominently features Jane and Finch as a "hotspot" of social problems and criminal activities, citizens and politicians alike will either call for or support initiatives pertaining to increased police presence and surveillance in the area, which in many cases also targets schools. The reasoning behind these initiatives varies. As indicated above, the media's "code-words" crystallize certain assumptions and presumed sets of behavioural traits for specific segments of the Canadian population. In the case of Jane and Finch, the area has become synonymous with Black people despite its heterogeneous population. And in light of the historical and deeply entrenched stigmatization of how Black bodies are often read (i.e., as lawless and aggressive troublemakers), surveillance is seen both as a pre-emptive measure and as a source of containment. Indeed, as scholars have emphasized, communities that are subjected to increased forms of police surveillance will undoubtedly experience disproportionate numbers of offences and arrests, resulting in a self-fulfilling prophecy (Henry and Tator 2006; James 2008; Mensah 2010; Wortley 2008). Interestingly, the *Toronto Star,* which at times has reported on the "deviant" behaviours of Black people, recently reminded us that, compared to their White counterparts, Blacks in Toronto are three times more likely to be stopped and documented by the Toronto Police (Rankin 2010). Obviously, this has relevance to how we come to understand the social issues in the Jane-Finch neighbourhood, because what often gets lost in the media and surveillance reports is how racial profiling, "cultural" differences, social and political neglect, lack of affordable housing and deepening polarities of wealth and poverty are *not* used to explain the circumstances of both individual members and their communities. Neither is attention given to the structural processes of inequity, which largely shape individuals' marginal positions.

A third point that might render Jane and Finch unique in the Canadian lexicon is the hierarchical and racialized place and space given to Black migrants. Historically, Canada has had a preference for White immigrants, who were perceived to be easily assimilated into the English or French racial population. Until the 1960s, many Black immigrants to Canada came as domestics and service workers (frequently on temporary work visas and/or permits). Vilna Bashi explains that Canada's historical anti-Black immigration policy was mitigated in large part by the "idea that admitting Blacks meant the nation was just asking for problems (i.e., race riots) that Britain and the U.S. had to bear for having Black residents" (Bashi 2004: 585–586). However, even though since 1967 the majority of immigrants to Canada are admitted on a stringent point system (which favours skilled, independent and highly educated migrants), the racialization of the Jane-Finch community may very well signal the growth rates, demographic shifts and permanent succeeding generations of racialized people that Canada's immigration policies, legislation and practices have long tried to prevent. In many ways, discourses about immigrants and refugees generally, and Blacks in particular, have yet to adequately surmount (or go beyond) problematic and racist references pertaining to whether "they" can be sufficiently like "us." These tensions often expose the limitations of Canada's multicultural policies and posturing.

Finally, it is important to note that the discourses around the Jane-Finch community obscure (or are buffered by) a seeming national disinterest toward the historically segregated and the systematically marginalized treatment of Aboriginal communities. Briefly, the reasons may vary, as Aboriginal communities might be perceived as either already "regulated" (as per ongoing colonization) or beyond what is "possible." Furthermore, there is no denying that racialization and criminalization account for the conditions of the communities in which Aboriginals live, learn, work and play. These conditions are influenced by our ambivalence about the place of immigrants and marginalized people in our social, economic and cultural development, and our obsession with who are likely to make good neighbours in terms of property value, the level of academic success of the neighbourhood school and the children with whom our children will be mixing at school and in the neighbourhood.

Essentially, over the years, Jane and Finch has served an exemplar of the social and economic problems and related activities that plague Canadian society, and can similarly serve to inform us of the issues, concerns, experiences and aspirations of members of that community. But are the problems that plague communities such as Jane and Finch, sometimes for generations, solely the responsibility of the residents? In the case of immigrants, would it be true to say that, despite their "immigrant dream" of a better life in Canada and what Canada purports to represent for them and their children, once established in Canada, they conveniently put aside their aspirations? What accounts for the young people's reportedly poor schooling and educational participation, their underperformance and disengagement from school, despite the many supports and remedial programs established by education administrators and governments?

Conclusion

I remain persuaded that parents living in Jane and Finch, just like parents living in middle-class communities, are concerned with the welfare of their children in terms of their gaining the educational and employment opportunities that will make them productive and successful Canadians. As such, with education as the only (socially sanctioned) route to satisfying these ambitions, it is understandable that parents and children would look to schools to provide the necessary teaching and learning that ensures educational success.

But the dominant or familiar narrative concerning these communities is that they are incubators of trouble and violence and offer a limited perspective of the opportunities that can be gained in life. As such, they are thought of as places to avoid and from which to escape. This suggests there is a much-needed counter-narrative that will expose the ways in which societal structures (i.e., economic, political, social, cultural, judicial, collectively) create, regulate and sustain unequal relationships within society that are evident in school policies, programs and practices. The counter-narrative must also tell of how students, as early as elementary school, continue to be confined to educational institutions and systems that struggle, and are failing, to recognize their inherent abilities and potential, as well as their hopes. Ultimately, what Jane and Finch has come to signify speaks more about a world that is not yet fair, humane or caring.

Notes

1. While the same question has been raised in the wake of the August 2011 riots in Britain, we have not seen politicians, government agencies or media appraising the social conditions and employment opportunities for youth in the area. However, there have always been ongoing concerns about the educational performance and outcome of students. In this regard, there have been continuing remedial school programs. As well, concern about gangs and criminal activities makes the community one that is consistently patrolled by police.

2. Out of the 232 shooting incidents in Toronto, approximately eleven incidents occurred in the Jane-Finch area between August and December 2005. For a breakdown of individual shootings see: <canadafreepress.com/gun-shootings-toronto-2005.htm>.

3. *Star Phoenix* [Saskatoon], "Canadian Soccer Skills Need Polish," August 7, 2007. At <canada.com/story_print.html?id=e00f234b-3b07-4dd1-ae68-d7e16af6cbc8&sponsor=>.

Chapter 2

Jane and Finch – A Profile

Two major roads, Jane Street and Finch Avenue, meet in the northwestern corner of Toronto. It is at this intersection (as some residents say in jest: "the widest intersection in the world") that some 75,000 people of various ethnic, racial, religious and generational backgrounds intermingle, living, working and playing with and among each other. If you stand on the corner you will see people of seemingly every ethnic, racial and religious background. Some are in traditional dress — Muslim women in flowing *chadors;* Ghanaian women in colourful *kente* dresses with their heads wrapped in a matching print; elderly Sri Lankan women in simple saris and elderly Italian widows dressed in black. There are men and women in suits or casual wear, on their way to or from work. Most people are in jeans, the staple North American garment. All go about their business along the busy streets, indifferent to the make-up of the neighbourhood, something that has become a mere fact of life.[1]

Two malls take up two corners of the quadrant formed by the intersection of Jane Street and Finch Avenue. In the northwest corner, Yorkgate Mall, built in 1990, houses a public health clinic, a Seneca College campus and the York University–TD Community Engagement Centre. The eponymous Jane-Finch Mall in the southeast corner was constructed more than thirty years ago. Both malls border side streets that are lined with detached and semi-detached houses, maze-like townhouse complexes and towering highrises. Norfinch Shopping Centre, which, despite its name, is a small strip mall, and a gas station are located on the southwest corner. In the northeast corner is a cluster of three highrise buildings at 5, 10 and 25 San Romanoway. Two of the buildings are eighteen floors high and the other has thirty-three floors, one of which (number 5) is a condominium. These buildings, clustered together on a grassy field, have about 892 units that house approximately 4,400 residents. Of these, 2,800 — over half — are children and youth. The many highrises mean that the community is densely populated. Indeed, with approximately 80,000 people living within a few kilometres of the "intersection,"[2] it is.

If you travel about three long blocks north on Jane Street, or east on Finch Avenue, you will come across roads leading to York University. In fact, Canada's third-largest university is northeast of Jane and Finch, and a neighbour of the community. In early 2009, when some people considered what might be done to address the negative reputation of the neighbourhood, one suggestion was to change its name to "University Heights." Community members sneered. Among other things, their reactions reflected the ambivalent relationship that the community has long had with the university.[3]

A major meeting place at Jane and Finch is its malls. These are not just places of trade or shopping. Residents, particularly those who live in the apartment buildings, gather there. These spaces are a place where goods are attained but also where community ties are built and refashioned. In the early morning, before most shopkeepers have opened up, the malls are taken over by retired Italian men who roam their walkways, animatedly conversing in their mother tongue. They live with their families in the semi-detached homes with carefully tended vegetable gardens, well-manicured lawns and the occasional bird fountain. The now rarely used bocce ball courts on the grounds of local Catholic schools and local parks offer a faint reminder that the schools were once teeming with these men's children. Most are grown and have long since moved away, many to Woodbridge, the newer Italian suburban enclave north of Toronto. While a large number of single-family homes in the area are still owned by these older Italian immigrants, the population continues to change. African, Caribbean, South Asian and Asian migrants have begun to buy the homes that come up for sale in the community. And the presence of this diversity and buying power is felt in the shopping districts as well.

Jane-Finch Mall has a Shoppers Drug Mart and a CIBC bank branch. However, for the most part, it is made up of small businesses almost exclusively owned and operated by racial minorities. These stores — a West Indian grocery store, an African hair salon, an Indian jewellery stall, a jerk chicken takeout spot, a kiosk selling international calling cards — serve the specific tastes and needs of a diverse immigrant community. The mall is generally a lively place, but Sunday is the day that it is liveliest, when a boisterous flea market takes over. With struggling room only, it is a packed, energetic event where Hindi music blares from the portable stereos, and crowds browse the stalls that sell Jamaican reggae music and dancehall movies, knock-off Louis Vuitton purses, Bollywood DVDs, parakeets, African music and films and various cultural foods, as well as more mundane household and fashion items and toys.

In the long summer days, on the lawns surrounding the buildings in the various neighbourhoods of the community, children dart in and out of the shadows cast by the forest of highrises that try, vainly, to block out the sun. And it is like a scene from other parts of the city. Punjabi children slip down the slides, watched over by elderly Sikh men in turbans and *shalwar kameez* who have gathered under the trees to talk. Young Vietnamese couples, wearing flip-flops and free-flowing trousers likely purchased from Jane-Finch Mall, take leisurely walks and push their young children in strollers. One can hear *hijabi* Somali girls shriek and laugh as they are chased by their little brothers. Pulsing hip-hop music floats from an apartment window, offering itself as a sound track. The peaceful tone of summer evenings in Jane and Finch belies the intensity and complexity of the community's storied past — and present. This is a place where Toronto's fears about race, poverty and violence intersect.

About five townhouse complexes are located around the intersection. Many of them are Toronto Community Housing Corporation (TCHC) social housing properties. They can be easily spotted because they lack the tell-tale signs of ownership: carefully tended gardens, garbage-free lawns, new windows, freshly painted front doors and bird baths. The maze of townhouses is painted a yellow-beige colour, which has proven to be a rather tempting canvas for graffiti artists. Austere iron railings separate the frontages of these row houses. On Jane Street, there is a group of buildings that are cut off from the rest of the area's sights and sounds by a network of small lanes. These buildings have been named "Connections." It is an ironic name, since they connect to nothing but each other. The other large TCHC townhouse complex on Driftwood Avenue, a street that runs off of Finch parallel to Jane, is known as "Lane," which locals also know as "Top Lane" and "Bottom Lane" (officially Grandravine).[4]

A significant number of highrise apartment buildings — some with as many as 427 units, reaching as high as thirty-three floors — dot the area. McGahan (1995: 227) argues that highrise apartment buildings, whether luxury-style or social housing, work against creating community. Unlike single-family homes, which offer their residents self-expression through "manipulation of their dwellings," apartment dwellers all live behind the same doors, allowing for less evaluation of each other as neighbours. Thus, a distance is created even as the lack of physical distance creates other problems: joint walls, floors and ceilings mean hearing, smelling and knowing quite a bit about the neighbours, whether one wants to or not. This excess of information, unwillingly shared, keeps people wary of those who may know too much about them and about whom possibly distasteful things are known. The need for privacy or the management of relationships means handing over control and autonomy: "High-rise tenants are... more dependent on agents of formal authority to secure order; strong reliance is placed on the superintendent to mediate relationships among them" (McGahan 1995: 228). It may be argued that in Jane and Finch the effect of these highrise buildings, particularly in light of the crowding they create, is a demand for more intervention from social housing authorities or even the police. However, this is not a reflection on the people who live in them, but rather a logical result of a residential structure that promotes anonymity even as it presses people together.

Because of its high density, concentration of racial and ethnic minorities, low-income housing, gangs, drug problems and violence, Jane and Finch is often viewed as Canada's equivalent to an American ghetto (see O'Grady, Parnaby and Schikschneit 2010). In December 2002, a report of the Jane-Finch Street Involved Youth Issues Coalition indicated that Jane-Finch has "one of the highest proportions of youth, sole-supported families, refugees and immigrants, low-income earners and public housing tenants of any community in Toronto" (MacNevin 1999: 236–237). However, it is worth noting that, despite the cluster of subsidized highrise apartments and townhouses, the area is *not* dominated by social housing. It is estimated that there are a significant number of market rent units among the semi-detached homes, townhouses, highrises and condominiums. Williams and Clarke (2003) report that about a third of all Toronto Community Housing Corporation's developments in the area known as North York are found in Jane and Finch, and today, 80 percent of the area's housing is not subsidized.

Jason (pseudonym) recently bought a home in the area. Soon after he moved in, an elderly White neighbour approached him.

"Are you the new owner?" she asked.

"Yes," he replied.

"Welcome to the neighbourhood! Don't listen to all that bad talk about it," she urged. "This is a good area. I've lived here forty years. When I came, there were only two houses on this road."

Of course, Jason already agreed with his neighbour, having grown up in the area himself. Now a professional, he chose to buy a home that is about a two-minute stroll to the intersection of Jane Street and Finch Avenue, and its lively mall. Like the people of the community, its architecture and spatial organization has surprising international correlates.

The philosophy behind the urban planning that went into designing the low-income housing in Jane and Finch was borrowed from the Swiss-French architect Le Corbusier's famous concept of the "tower in the park." His vision of a city of tall towers in park settings became the inspiration for addressing the housing needs of the urban poor "by building up instead of out." However, as Caldwell (2005) notes, there were inherent problems with this design:

> Soaring apartments, he thought, would finally give sunlight and fresh air to city laborers, who had been trapped in narrow and fetid back streets since the dawn of urbanization. But high-rise apartments mixed badly with something poor communities generate in profusion: groups of young, armed, desperate males.

In the wake of the 2005 riots in France by disaffected racialized youth in the Paris *banlieues* (government-built public housing), the architectural ideas of Le Corbusier garnered renewed attention.

According to Wacquant (2008: 5), it is in the French working-class *banlieues* that one finds a "fundamentally heterogeneous population according to ethno-provenance (and secondarily, class position), whose isolation is mitigated by the strong presences of public institutions catering to social needs." Caldwell writes that some Americans are quite anxious to point out the difference between American suburbs, havens for the White middle-class and increasingly gated, and the Paris *banlieues*, populated by Arab, African and South Asian immigrants and their French-born children. While Americans may take some refuge in the differences between the American and French suburbs that contribute to the alienation of youth, Canadians might do well to consider the architectural, demographic and social similarities of Jane and Finch to the Paris *banlieues*. Indeed, Jane and Finch, with its diverse population and many social agencies, clearly has much in common with the *banlieue*. And as Graff (2005) contends, "the grimy, soulless suburban apartment blocks that ring France's big cities" have much in common with the bleak, grubby highrises that dominate the Jane-Finch community.

It was in the 1960s that Jane and Finch was established as a community with public housing to accommodate a low-income and growing immigrant population (see also Hall 2008; MacNevin 1999; Richardson 2008). The population growth was rapid, particularly through immigration, from 1,300 people in 1961 to 33,000 in 1971, and continual increases since then (Sakamoto 1986). Doucet (1999: 19) notes that "traditionally, an immigrant reception area, characterized by a large stock of affordable housing and proximity to both public transit and jobs that were suitable for recent arrivals, emerged within the inner-city areas of most North American cities." This area in Toronto was Kensington Market, between College and Dundas Streets in downtown Toronto. However, as Doucet notes, this changed in the 1970s as "the immigrant reception area has moved upward and outward" to neighbourhoods that would traditionally be regarded as the suburbs, or today might be termed the "in-between suburbs" (Ibid.). This movement outward continues as the suburbs outside of Toronto have begun to see a tremendous influx of new immigrants. Despite this, Jane and Finch remains an immigrant reception area.

The demographics of Jane and Finch could easily serve to map the changes in Canada's immigration policies and global refugee patterns. Until the 1960s, the area was populated largely by Italians. In the 1960s and 1970s, the area received Black women arriving alone from the Caribbean to work as domestics and, later, other family members — including their children. Vietnamese, many escaping Asian refugee camps, arrived there from 1979 to 1994. And, most recently, Somalis fleeing years of civil strife in their homeland have settled in the area. With changes to Canada's immigration policies in the 1960s, Jane and Finch has been the destination of many immigrants from all parts of the world, particularly from regions other than Europe. According to the 2006 Census, there were 9,900 recent immigrants in the area, about 39 percent from South Asia (India, Pakistan, etc.); 16 percent from South America; 12 percent from Africa (mostly West Africa, with about 8 percent); 11 percent from Western Central Asia and the Middle East; 9 percent from Southeast Asia (including the Philippines); and 6 percent from the Caribbean and Bermuda. Black people, most of them born in Canada of Caribbean parents, made up the largest racial minority group in the area — that is, 20 percent out of the 71 percent racial minority population. South Asians at 18 percent are the next largest racial minority group, followed by Latin Americans and South Asians at approximately 9 percent each. However, the largest racial group is by far Whites, with 29 percent. They were less likely to live in Jane and Finch's social housing highrises and townhouses (City of Toronto 2008).

It is estimated that the immigrant residents of Jane and Finch are from over seventy-two countries and speak about 120 languages (little wonder, then, that some people in their blogs have described Jane and Finch as "Toronto's most multicultural area"). In *Jane-Finch: Priority Area Profile*, the City of Toronto (2008) identifies the community's top twelve languages:

1. Italian — 6555
2. Spanish — 5330
3. Vietnamese — 4835
4. Punjabi — 3075
5. Urdu — 2270
6. Tamil — 1470
7. Chinese (no dialect) — 1410
8. Arabic — 1375
9. Gujarati — 1165
10. Chinese-Cantonese — 1135
11. Somali — 910
12. Akan-Twi — 875

Despite this diversity, media coverage disproportionately features Black people in its portrayals of the area. This is probably because the lurid coverage is intended to evoke images of American ghettos and racial division as opposed to a more "Canadian" vision of multiculturalism, however flawed. Furthermore, as Murdie and Teixeira (2000: 217) point out, in the absence of enclaves of successful immigrants to help them integrate into Canadian society, many recent immigrants from the Caribbean, Latin American and Africa tend to remain in transitional communities such as Jane and Finch. They note that "pockets of concentration of Caribbean immigrants (often in public housing) have been identified in both the inner city and the suburbs of Montreal and Toronto." And they go on to add that "it is important to reiterate that none of these areas of concentration can be described as a ghetto, since they do not resemble the large-scale ghettos that characterize many U.S. cities."

The "Corridor"

The word "corridor" is popularly used, some people would say, and invented by the media to describe the Jane-Finch community, particularly in relation to Jane Street, which is lined with many highrise buildings. Other words for corridor are "passageway," "hallway" and "walkway." Hence, the use of "corridor" to describe Jane and Finch might conjure up a space that is like a long, narrow hallway, darkened by the crush of claustrophobia-inducing highrise buildings that sprout by the roadsides. This corridor is hemmed in by major roads, a highway, middle-class communities and a ravine that separates it from York University.[5] The description has socio-economic import, too. Corridors are spaces that one passes through to get from one place to another — not a space in which to linger, spend time or live. Further, insofar as a corridor is an enclosed space that can only (or mainly) be accessed by doorways and is only a travel space (or walkway), then people who choose to remain in such a space for any length of time might be people who are content to live in a space that limits their opportunities and possibilities, or might be those who wish to use the space to engage in activities that they would not be able to engage in elsewhere. There is also the sense in which a corridor serves as a place of banishment to accommodate individuals that we wish to "put out of sight and out of mind," sometimes as a form of punishment. Here, we think of "bad" students sent from class out into the hallway or corridor of a school. It seems the media subscribes to such thinking. They use the metaphor to depict the community as one in which people are trapped in a narrow space with limited exit routes and hopeless conditions, and with people who engage in antisocial and violent activities.

In fact, the head of a local community agency made this point to a reporter. Under the headline "Corridor of power: Community organizers turn negative perceptions into positive results in the troubled Jane-Finch area," Mendez Berry (2000: 11) quotes the agency worker as saying, "Jane-Finch has been stigmatized by media portrayals that consistently dwell on the negative, and has also been the victim of a lack of social services and infrastructure." In an earlier *Globe and Mail* article with the headline "Jane-Finch slaying caught on videotape," reporter Natalie Southworth (2000: A18) wrote about the "long record of violence in the troubled Jane-Finch corridor." The accompanying photograph of the shooting site from a security camera had a caption that read: "The parking lot at Jane Street and Eddystone Avenue, in the Jane-Finch area, where two men were shot on July 24. Police say they have videotape showing the gunman fleeing the scene on a mountain bike. The tape also shows witnesses standing by while the shootings took place." Readers might have interpreted this to mean that Jane-Finch residents are not simply victims of the violence occurring in their neighbourhoods, but complicit in it through their apathy and indifference. So while witnesses to crime in other parts of the city may stand by "in shock," a message implicit in the article is that people in Jane and Finch are so desensitized to violence that they stand by doing nothing.

In June 2001, the CBC nightly news program *The National* showed a now infamous twenty-minute documentary called *Street Rappers.* The documentary followed a rap group based in Jane and Finch called the Smugglas. Rife with images of drug use, drinking, swaggering, gunshot scars and profanity, the documentary caused an uproar. The community was horrified by the national airing of a highly selective, stereotyped depiction of where they live, learn, work and play. The documentary seemed to have been designed to evoke American ghetto stereotypes, depicting only Black people, despite the area's diversity. The documentary's producers protested that the documentary "was never meant to mirror all of the texture and complexity of the Jane-Finch neighbourhood" but was instead "a reflection of how they [the Smugglas] see their neighbourhood" (Higgins 2001: 1).[6] However, Smugglas rapper Infinite suggests there was a definite agenda, arguing that the CBC production team characterized him as a "gangsta rapper" despite his emphasis on his work with youth in schools.

Even as the media attempt to present "positive" portraits of the community, or "look deeper" into it, they often reinforce the very ideas they claim to want to counteract. And, the message tends to be about the importance of an individual's efforts and not about how systemic inequity limits the opportunities that might have helped individuals to better their situation. In fact, such an individual's efforts are complicated by the media's habit of cultivating a menacing image though the spread of unfair, disturbing headlines and articles. And this slant re-inscribes the reputation of Jane and Finch as tough, violent and harmful, a place from which it is difficult to escape. Take, for example, the *Toronto Star*'s articles about Richard Asante and Alwyn Barry.

The *Toronto Star* featured an article about the draft of twenty-two-year-old Richard Asante to Major League Soccer, Toronto FC. The article was punctuated with references to Asante's residence in the Jane-Finch area, slanting toward a rags-to-riches story — although the article did note that, as a rookie, Asante had yet to make big money. The sub-headline read: "Grew up in a rough area, studied at Syracuse University and he's now set to lace up for MLS team" (Campbell 2007). Asante was described as "the son of a refugee from Ghana" who had "risen from one of Toronto's toughest neighbourhoods to earn a soccer scholarship to Syracuse University." Asante was the only Toronto resident to be drafted to the Toronto team, but the article's focus is on the part of the city he comes from, segregating him from any larger citizenship: "They live in a brick townhouse on Driftwood Ave., just off Jane St., half a kilometre north of Finch Ave., and they're aware of the area's violent reputation." But reporter Campbell did go on to say, "When Asante thinks about growing up on Driftwood, he doesn't think of crime. Instead, he remembers how living in an area with so many other Ghanaian families eased his transition to life in Canada."

In 2007, Alwyn Barry, eighteen, made a seven-minute film documenting his battle against colon cancer with Shoot With This, an after-school film program run by the Toronto District School Board (TDSB). An obituary article that appeared in the *Toronto Star* after he succumbed to his illness quotes a TDSB social worker who worked with him on the film: "'He was bright. He was articulate. He was from a two-parent family,' Blackwood said of his protégé from the Jane-Finch neighbourhood of northwest Toronto. 'He was the one guy who could have changed people's ideas about Jane-Finch (being only about guns and drugs)'" (Goddard 2007: A6). Barry's poignant struggle with cancer received much attention because of his mission to counter Jane and Finch's stigma and the media's fascination with exemplars. Barry was constructed as someone set apart from other youth in the area, being "bright," "articulate" and from "a two-parent family." While he is presented as a shining example of initiative, courage and talent, like Asante, he was also viewed as an exception — the very thing Barry would probably have argued that he was not. Barry, like many Jane-Finch residents who sought to counter the stereotypes, was unwillingly drafted into their reinforcement. Even the account of his tragic and untimely death seemed to imply the hopelessness of the crusade to change the perceptions of hearts and minds.

News reporters visit the area like bemused doctors who only see the patient when there is an illness, looking for a diagnosis of what ails the community. Jane and Finch's complicated struggle with image and truth, perception and reality, is best captured by the headline that has had so much to do with its fame, or infamy. "Can anything good come out of this place?" it demands in John Barber's (1999) *Globe and Mail* article. Possibly Fleras is correct when he says that media coverage of Jane and

Finch is not only about the geographic space, but about the lives of racial minorities. Fleras (1995: 414) writes:

> Mass media portrayals of aboriginal and racial minorities are as likely to inform and reveal (if selectively) as they are to misinform, conceal, and evade. There is no shortage of examples about information whose one-sidedness borders on propaganda. How often does media coverage of the Jane-Finch corridor in Greater Toronto veer outside the confines of a high-density concrete jungle composed mostly of African-Canadians immersed in drugs and guns?

The "Year of the Gun"

This "troubled community" was further enshrined as a place of fighting and gang activity in 2005 when gun-related violence peaked initially in the summer months, earning it the media title, the "summer of the gun." As the gun incidents stretched through the summer, 2005 became the "year of the gun." The year before, homicides in Toronto had totalled sixty-eight, but by the end of 2005, the total number was seventy-eight, with fifty-two of these involving guns. As the city's alarm grew, public and media pressure was put on the mayor to increase police presence and resources. This resulted in the Toronto Police Services Board recruiting some 150 new police officers, but interestingly no officers were recruited from the Jane-Finch area.[7] Actually, as the *Toronto Star*'s Daniel Dale (2010) reports, "The police made no hires the whole decade [2000–2009] from one postal code in the Jane St. and Sheppard Ave. W. area. The force hired only four people from Lawrence Heights" (a mid-city community with somewhat similar demographics and issues to that of Jane and Finch).

Some of those summer murders took place in Jane and Finch. Most did not. Regardless, Jane and Finch once again stood as an easily identifiable centre of a ubiquitous problem. After weeks of seeming helplessness in the face of murder after murder, police reported the arrest of about forty "gang members" on weapons-related charges. The initial reporting of the arrests garnered a sort of jubilance in the wake of a long period when police seemingly did nothing to stop gun crimes. First reports announced it as the busting of a "Jane-Finch gang." Later reports indicated that the gang members were from Rexdale — a similar "at-risk" community over four kilometres west of Jane and Finch and physically separated by a major highway and train tracks. Little was made of the error linking the gang to Jane and Finch. This gaffe reflects a common practice of the media (as assisted by the police) of portraying the community as being Toronto's most crime-ridden. And if crime occurs in areas within a certain radius of the Jane-Finch intersection, it is commonly described as having happened "close to the Jane-Finch area." Assumedly, this serves to give listeners, viewers and readers a "known" and already defined reference point. Such a practice serves to both comfort and alarm. The comfort is that crime is not rampant in the city but contained within a distant, poor neighbourhood. The alarm is that such an area exists at all and that area residents, and the violence they carry with them, might encroach upon the city.

On Boxing Day of 2005, the violence *did* encroach upon the city. On that day, there was a shooting on a busy downtown main street, crowded with holiday shoppers. News reports indicate that six bystanders and one potential suspect were shot as two groups exchanged gunfire. The outrage following the incident was even more telling than previous media reports about where in Toronto violence is expected to occur. The death of one innocent bystander, fifteen-year-old Jane Creba, out shopping with her family, inflamed a city shocked and terrified that gun violence had finally spilled over onto supposedly "safe" turf. One Jane-Finch resident noted in a local television (CityTV) interview that he was used to seeing such violence in his own neighbourhood but not in the city centre. Ironically, it was he, a Jane-Finch resident, who said what so many were thinking: shootings happen in certain neighbourhoods, which is upsetting, but little cause for alarm. The reaction to the downtown shooting indicates that when gun violence leaves the neighbourhoods where it is expected to occur and invades places anyone could be, including the privileged, then people will be horrified. Toronto mayor David Miller summed up people's heightened dismay when he said: "It's like a shooting happening in your house and that's how everyone has reacted" (Gray 2005: A7).

The *Toronto Star* quoted Creba's school principal as saying that she was "a beloved student, a top scholar, an incredibly talented athlete. In many respects this was a role model to teenagers everywhere" (Carniol and Teotonio 2005: A01). The tragedy of this young girl's death is indisputably enormous. But the media machine quickly made it clear that, not only was she innocent, she was also valuable. Of course she was valuable; the problem is that so many of the city's other gun-related deaths yielded victims that were made to seem less so. As *Toronto Star* reporter Rosie DiManno terms them, the "urban savages" usually shoot those who are like themselves. On Christmas Eve of that same year, Cordell Charles Skinner, age twenty-five, was shot in Jane and Finch outside a local daycare centre. There was some requisite outrage because Skinner was a father, and the shooting was outside a daycare. But that daycare was located in a public housing property in the Jane-Finch area, and for the most part, Christmas was celebrated without too much public horror.[8] Also, there was no outcry in August 2005 when four-year-old Shaquan Cadougan was hit by bullets (allegedly meant for his fifteen-year-old basketball-star brother) in a drive-by shooting. His brother has since left the neighbourhood, moving to the Unites States with the promise of a basketball scholarship and success — another example of a "hero" and hope.

The Boxing Day killing of Jane Creba dispelled the comfort that the containment of violence "over there" offered. DiManno refers to this containment when she asked in her *Toronto Star* (2005: A06) column: "For how many years have we been telling anyone who would listen — most especially one another — that sporadic murders and a few neighbourhoods stricken by chronic violence did not characterize the city as a whole?" Nevertheless, it had been quite easy for reporters and others to dismiss those few stricken neighbourhoods, Jane and Finch among them. In acknowledging the "far away" neighbourhoods, DiManno continued: "We certainly should worry for distant neighbours, who cannot just shut the door to keep out violence. It follows them inside; it strangles their households." But this cursory sympathy is followed by the real problem or concern: "And there is always, as was proven Boxing Day, the chance — however slim — the gunfire will come to us, in our shared communal spaces, to our innocent children, a parent rushing past with shopping bags in hand, an off-duty police officer." It is this chance that feeds the drive to demonize rather than understand the "urban savages." Fear begets anger, which begets simplistic knee-jerk accusations and disgust. DiManno ridicules those who would critique her characterization of the shooters as "urban savages": "the hug-a-thug crowd won't have us demonize these poor, misbegotten youth, so 'victimized' by the root causes of their own misanthropy — Prime Minister Paul Martin, without any supporting evidence at hand, yesterday described Monday's dreadful incident as a tragedy and 'consequence of exclusion.'"

Prime Minister Paul Martin visited the Jane-Finch area on November 9, 2005, following the outcry over the summer of shootings that stretched into fall and in the wake of the riots in Paris, France. Martin toured a local school, community centre and housing complex, announcing $50 million in funding for community agencies working against guns and gang violence and for youth justice projects. He also referred to the coming announcement of changes to the Criminal Code that would increase mandatory minimum sentencing for gun-related crimes. In further attempts to address underlying causal factors for the violence, $1.9 million was committed to providing opportunities for youth to acquire employment skills (*Y-life* 2005). While this visit yielded great largesse for community agencies, it also brought further notoriety. The Prime Minister's visit served to re-confirm Jane and Finch as a national symbol of crime, poverty and violence.

Reaction in the community was mixed, with some applauding the employment funding and others concerned about the repercussions of mandatory minimum sentences for youth. And with the spectre of the Paris riots also looming in the background, the *Globe and Mail* ran the following headline above an article by Joe Friesen (2005: A14): "Despair and frustration at Jane and Finch: Area could explode in violence unless root causes tackled, community warns." Friesen quoted Margaret Parsons, the executive director of the African-Canadian Legal Clinic, as declaring that

> the area is a tinderbox that could explode in violence, just like the Paris suburbs did over the past few weeks. "It could easily erupt," she said. "We can look at Paris as an example and prevent this from happening [but] I think the sense of despair, I think the sense of hopelessness, the sense of frustration [are all present]."

Friesen reported that some young residents had told him that they felt the same way as the youth in Paris. One eighteen-year-old was quoted as saying: "There's a possibility of it happening here…. That's how we feel about it. It could be a threat." Roger Rowe, an African-Canadian lawyer living in the area, was also quoted by Anthony Rienhart (2005: A1) in the *Globe and Mail* as saying that the Paris riots were a possibility if the privileged, among whom he counts himself, remain disengaged from the area. The article, "He could live anywhere, but Jane-Finch is home," which profiled Rowe, was seemingly an attempt to show that "good" people also live in the area. In so doing, it called attention to Rowe's practice and residence in the area, as well as to the fact that his three children attended school there. Reinhart noted that with his credentials, Rowe could live anywhere: "Indeed he does — not in Rosedale or High Park or the Annex, but in Jane-Finch, Toronto's ground zero for gun violence." In this way, Reinhart emphasized Rowe's impressive commitment to the area, while also expressing incredulity that anyone who does not have to live in Jane-Finch would chose to reside there.

A Place of Transition

As mentioned earlier, living in Jane and Finch is often conceived by out-siders, and many residents, as temporary. It is a place where immigrants or first- and/or second-generation Canadians settle as they work on their move to the suburbs. Or it is where they are content to live in government-assisted housing until they can earn and/or save enough money to buy their first house or condominium at a reasonable or affordable price to move on and "move up." This transitory process is often described as "invasion-succession," where newcomers replace previous groups who have gained social upward mobility and moved outward spatially (Murdie and Ghosh 2010: 295).

For many of the residents of Jane and Finch, the terms "low income" and "lower class," despite their sociological application, move beyond a description of economic status to encompass a commentary on standards, habits and level of education. The people who live in Jane and Finch are not oblivious to these kinds of perceptions: in many ways, "getting out" of Jane and Finch has a lot to do with notions of class held by society at large rather than the realities of an economic situation. For example, the idea that living in the suburbs is a marker of wealth is a well-entrenched principle. The myth of the suburbs as a place where you live when you have made it is so strong that it is seems like heresy to deny or pretend otherwise. Seemingly, living in a big and new, preferably detached, home in a suburb is a universal motivator. How, then, can we object to someone — especially an immigrant, minority Canadian, or someone from a family who has lived in assisted housing for generations — wishing to own a bigger house in the suburb in which to raise children, rather than doing so in an apartment or condominium building in a "troubled," stigmatized community? Arguably, owning your own home in stigmatized Jane and Finch carries less personal value than living in subsidized housing in outer suburban areas that are assumed to be middle class. Besides, while the low property values make owning a home attractive and affordable, some homeowners complain of difficulty in selling when they wish to.

Trevor's (pseudonym) mother was one of those parents who wished to raise her son in a suburban community. As twenty-two-year-old Trevor (Personal communication, June 2009) recalled:

> I was approximately ten or eleven when my mother decided that we needed to move out of the community. We lived in the Jane and Finch community, starting in one of the government complexes (known as the Lane) then we moved to an apartment building. Being a single parent, I believe my mother wanted to do anything in her power to ensure that I would not become another statistic, or fall into the too-common stereotype of a Black youth. She decided that we would move up north into the growing [suburban] community [north of Toronto]. At the time we moved into the area… we were one of few Black families that lived in the suburban area which was mostly populated by Whites (mainly Italians).
>
> At my young age, I did not have an input on the move or where we were moving to. But I was comfortable with where we were living, and if we were going to move, I preferred to move to a community such as Brampton. My reason was that it was the

area where most of my family and friends who decided to leave Jane and Finch were moving to.

We moved in the summer when I was going into Grade 8, and I wanted to finish off my middle school at the school I attended from Grade. 6. I didn't think that I would be comfortable going to a new school for just one year. My mother agreed and we found a way for me to still attend my middle school. I believe we used the address of a friend or relative that still lived in that area. After finishing middle school, I had to attend a high school closer to by home.

In the film *How She Move* (2008), Annemarie Morais, who grew up in Jane and Finch, tells of the role that "stepping" played in the lives of a competitive dance group from the area. Stepping is an African-American dance form that blends traditional African movement with modern footwork and percussive dance that was popularized by African-American fraternities and sororities in the United States. While the film's setting is not Jane and Finch (because production costs meant they had to film it in Hamilton, Ontario, and all Canadian references were cut when the film was distributed in the U.S.), the gritty highrises and dismal urbanity shown are clearly meant to reflect the realities of the Jane-Finch area. The film's protagonist, Raya Green, is forced to return to the area when money runs out for her tuition to Seaton Hall, a private school where she is studying, hoping to eventually become a doctor and get out of her impoverished neighbourhood. She ends up stepping competitively with the Jane Street Junta in attempts to earn prize money to help with tuition. Her parents are eager to see her rise above their standard of living and not so eager to see her step dancing. They view that social milieu as part of what led her older sister to drug abuse and death. The idea of leaving the neighbourhood to make good is one common to many dance and sports films, but *How She Move* also engages the "getting out" mindset so often applied to Jane and Finch, setting it up as a place from which to escape. Even as Raya's participation in stepping, despite her parents' disapproval, brings her cash, recognition and, most of all, a sense of "coming home," the world of stepping — however affirming — is tied to a neighbourhood that cannot be a destination. Stepping may have helped Raya on her journey and reminded her of her roots, but she is still on her way out. While much has been made of the film's Jane-Finch roots or ties, and as much as it celebrates the area, its people and its culture, it also takes for granted that if you can get out, you must.

But getting out of the 'hood and moving "up" to the suburbs is not without its struggles, especially when its residents' bodies are imbued with particular social and cultural meaning in relation to geography, space or context. In other words, the fact that Black bodies tend to be identified with the Jane-Finch area and related antisocial problems and unlawful behaviours means that they are not likely to be welcomed in new, middle-class suburban areas. For in the popular imagination, it is not the social conditions that influence the behaviours, aptitudes and capacities of individuals, but the *culture* (values, norms, ideas, etc.) into which they were born or socialized. That culture is perceived to operate in individuals as if it is inherent or biological. In this regard, suburban people would be loath to having former Jane and Finch residents as neighbours, fearing that they might bring their working-class habits to the neighbourhood. So when Blacks began moving to Brampton, the sprawling suburb northwest of Toronto, to buy new homes, the people of that city become nervous and concerned. Most interesting are the perceptions that the former Jane-Finch residents — here the Black people were read as all migrating from Jane and Finch — could only own their Brampton home through government assistance. Specifically, it was rumoured in the summer of 2007 that a relocation program was offering people from Jane and Finch from $5,000 to $10,000 to buy a home in Brampton.[9] The mayor, councillors and police chief had all received inquiries from people upset over the alleged program. The police chief acknowledged that the inquiries were motivated by bigotry and offered that "they are not all criminals who live in Jane and Finch. There's a lot of good people who live there" (Douglas 2007: 3).[10]

The issue was raised at an August 2007 Brampton City Council meeting during a discussion of criminal activities among youth in the city. In her attempt to dispel the rumour, the mayor, like the police chief, employed a strategy often used by those seeking to defend the area and its people: she pointed to individuals who might be considered "upstanding citizens." In this case, the mayor disclosed that the area's (Peel Region) deputy chief grew up in Jane and Finch. Upstanding citizens are often held up to convince the rest of the Greater Toronto Area (GTA) that good people can and do live in Jane and Finch. The outraged e-mails and the rumour mongers, one of whom the mayor admitted was a school principal, demonstrate the depth of antipathy held for the area and its residents. The palpable fear that "their" community might be deluged by former Jane-Finch residents indicates that little attempt was made to disguise the racism and classism of such sentiment. Here we see the interconnection of class and race in the expressed bigotry and in the perception that it was only a relocation program of monetary compensation that would make it possible for Jane-Finch residents to move to Brampton.

Ironically, as suburban areas become attractive because of "affordable" housing and communities are perceived to offer better living conditions (supposedly away from the violence and crimes), good schooling for children and evidence of having "made it" (as immigrants, minorities and working-class people), Jane and Finch will be less viable for its residents. It is a more centrally located community with extensive facilities, including libraries, accessible transit service, many schools within short walking distance, Seneca College and York University. Here is how one university student, of Métis and African-Jamaican heritage, described her experiences of growing up in Jane and Finch and moving to Brampton with her parents.

> I began school in Toronto, where my family and I lived for a short period of time.... Then we moved to Brampton, where I had to make quite an adjustment.... In Toronto, there had been all kinds of people.... Brampton was very different from this. It seemed like a whole new world. For the first time, I think, I began to feel different — I felt isolated.
>
> This new community my family and I became a part of was predominantly European... and consisted of middle-class people. These factors alone affected my perception of the world; coming as I had from a poor working-class environment where we had been surrounded by government housing and high-rise buildings. I was just not ready for this new "habitat." Unlike the friendly, warm community that I had been forced to leave behind, the people in Brampton were very private, and they seemed to share an agenda that was in many respects different from those in my old community. I was immersed in a totally different cultural setting. (James 2010a: 98–99)

"It's Home"

The "corridor" construction of the Jane-Finch community, coupled with the sensational "urban underclass framework" of the media (O'Grady, Parnaby and Schikschneit, 2010), depicts Jane and Finch as a dark, dangerous passageway, a deadly stretch that unlucky immigrants must travel to reach a "better" life in which they will live the immigrant or American Dream. A safe passage through the corridor means the residents, or their children, will move away from a place characterized by "trouble" — an area always under police surveillance, under teachers' scrutiny and feared by the rest of the city — to the peaceful suburbs. These depictions conceal the fact that, to some individuals, Jane and Finch is a place for which they have developed deep feelings of belonging and loyalty — a home. It is a home from which residents send the message to outsiders that they stand for peace and do live harmoniously with each other. This message is sent through the Peace Walk, held every June since 2005 (the "year of the gun," discussed above). Residents walk north from the intersection of Jane and Sheppard to a parking lot at the corner of Jane and Finch where they celebrate with music, food and other cultural activities. The neighbourhood is also a place where those who care to celebrate their ethnic heritage come together in the summers to do so. Celebrations include the Caribbean (formerly Caribana) Children's Carnival, part of the larger Caribbean festival held in downtown Toronto each year at the beginning of August, the Canadian Hispanic Day Parade and the Driftwood Annual Multicultural Festival.

Over a decade ago, *Toronto Star* reporter Michelle Sheppard visited Jane and Finch and spoke to residents regarding their feelings about living in the area. What she heard from the residents produced the headline: "Jane-Finch's bad reputation isn't justified, residents say: It's not dangerous, it's home, they say" (Sheppard 1997: B3). Indeed, residents' accounts of the area can be very divergent, some as sensational as media accounts, others highly defensive and positive. At the time of the prime minister's visit to the area (autumn of 2005), CBC reporter Mary Wiens went on a tour of the "real Jane/Finch" led by Paul Nguyen and rapper Blacus Ninjah. Wiens asked Blacus to take her where he would have liked to take the prime minister. Blacus eschews the label "Jane-Finch," opting to be more specific by using Driftwood, Shoreham, Connections and the Lane to refer to specific sections of Jane and Finch. He describes Driftwood: "This is Driftwood Avenue, right behind Driftwood Community Centre. And this is basically where we call the hood — the real hood, the ghetto." Blacus described Christmas in the area as different from how it is observed in the suburbs. "We are not even worried about gifts," he said. "We are just happy to see everybody, we are happy to be alive, you know what I'm saying? Because every Christmas something happens to somebody." He recalled that one of his peers had been shot and killed in a nightclub around Christmastime the previous year. Blacus saw these occurrences as lessons: "Those kinds of things make you get a good grasp on life and realize that you know you could be here today and gone tomorrow" (Wiens 2005).

For the most part, residents of Jane and Finch will acknowledge the issues that help to brand their community as "troubled" — troublesome behaviours, gun violence, gang fights[11] — and are prepared to put effort into addressing them so that they can live in a safe and dependable community. In fact, a recent edition of *Sway* magazine (2011: 36–42) featured articles on the Jane and Finch area in a seeming effort to demonstrate that, although the neighbourhood has been plagued by a "myriad of social issues" related to stigmatization, systemic racism, isolation and lack of family support, residents have been able to, as one resident was quoted as saying, free their minds and get out of "the mental jail that can hold you sometimes at Jane and Finch" (38). One of two brothers (both accomplished lawyers) who "grew up at Jane and Eddystone, right near the Jane and Finch Mall" but now live outside of the area, remarked that "people have these misconceptions about Jane and Finch, about parents and children not caring. But we understood what was expected of us, and we had people to support us — we had the church and each other" (42). The six one-page magazine articles illustrated the resilience, the determination and the hard work of current and former residents, especially the youth, to find their voices and realize their aspirations. A number of the articles referenced the social and educational programs that have operated to support the educational, art and creative talents of the young people. One program is Success Beyond Limits (SBL), which provides peer tutoring, mentoring, after-school and other in-school support programs to students in the area. One of its signature programs is a summer educational program held at York University for students transitioning from the two area middle schools to high school.

Members of the community, especially young residents, also expose the negative, perhaps hoping that through the process they can help to change its reputation so that "outsiders" come to see the community differently. For example, Nguyen created the website Jane-Finch.com in 2004 to contest negative media images of the area and to provide a forum for the voices of residents. Nevertheless, he also included Chuckie Akenz's (see note 6) rap video "You Got Beef," which presented images of some of the racial tensions that existed in the area. For Nyugen, images such as those in the video represent the reality of his community of which he was very proud. As he put it: "When you come here, you see a pho restaurant right beside a barber and braids hair shop…. It just shows the community exemplifying racial harmony and post-modernity. Most residents here are proud of this hard-working community" (Han Nguyen 2005).

The Real Toronto, an underground DVD that claims to show the gritty realities of Toronto's gang culture, enjoyed notoriety when it was released in October 2005. The director, a twenty-two-year-old Russian immigrant known only as the Madd Russian, portrayed Jane and Finch as one of Toronto's high-crime communities. He did not directly interview his subjects (most of whom concealed their identities with bandanas), but documented them flashing guns, trash talking and free-styling. It seems from the content of the DVD, and the excitement it engendered among young people upon its release, that gang culture is perceived as glamorous. While most residents, young and old, decried the sensationalized coverage that painted a negative picture of the area, others seemed at times to embrace it. This embrace might be a function of their resentment or bravado — a way of resisting the wider society's construction of the community. Or it could be as simple as youth finding a handy way into the toughness that some adolescent boys habitually adopt.

As home, Jane and Finch is for many of its residents a neighbourhood that, in the words of a former resident, is "filled with good people who have a lot to offer." And referring to his own and his brother's accomplishments as lawyers, he notes: "We're proof… that Jane and Finch is not all that bad" (*Sway* 2010: 42). But there is no denying that sometimes, despite the love for and commitment to home, it can and does become a space and place that cannot hold a person's desires and aspirations; nor can the everyday conditions allay the fears and anxieties of parents who, as all parents, wish for a safe, secure and peaceful neighbourhood where their children can live, learn and play. Take for instance, Trevor's mother, who insisted on moving out of the Jane-Finch neighbourhood because she did not want him, as he put it, to "become another statistic, or fall into the too-common stereotype of a Black youth." In reflecting on the move, Trevor now suggests that, while at the time he did not appreciate his mother's concern, he has since come to appreciate that his mother likely "made a smart decision":

> During my teenage years I couldn't see why my mother wanted to move away from the area we both grew up in. She used to say that it was a bad area, and that she wanted me to have access to the best education I could get and that she did not want me to fall into the stereotype. I couldn't understand her when I was younger, because both her and my uncle grew up in that area and they both became successes. Neither of them fell into the common stereotype of Black people, so I didn't think that I would. Now that I am older and have a better understanding of things, I feel that moving out of the Jane and Finch area may have been a good idea. Too many of the people I grew up with in that community have fallen between the cracks. Numerous people who I called friends when I was younger have become victims of murder, or have had someone in their family murdered, and others who I called my friends have fallen into a life of crime and have committed acts such as murder. I am not saying that if I stayed in that community I may have been inclined to crime, but I do believe my mom made a smart decision judging by how some of my friends who stayed in that area turned out. (Personal communication, June 2009)

Conclusion

I lived in a highrise building at Tobermory, "T-Block" as we call it, which is located one block east of the Jane and Finch intersection. Directly across the street to the south is the public library, and one block east is a recreation centre with a swimming pool. Many of the neighbourhood youth who participated in programs attend this centre. Our building consisted of low-income subsidized housing and a diverse set of residents with respect to age, race, family size and ancestry. There were residents who came from Eritrea, Ethiopia, Ghana, Nigeria, South Africa and Egypt. Many families that resided in the building were also from Jamaica, Trinidad and Dominica, and the list goes on. I also lived side by side with European families. Some families have lived in the building for a couple of generations. It was very much a vertical neighbourhood, a vertical mosaic painted with a global paintbrush.

That I lived on "T-Block" was more important than the fact we lived in Jane and Finch. Everyone had their little area that they claimed — whether it was Shoreham, Driftwood, Lane, Connections, Yellowstone or Tobermory — they all are collectively Jane and Finch but at the same time, they were not. There are multiple neighbourhoods, all with a story and an identity of their own that simultaneously made up and complicated Jane and Finch. (Sam Tecle, Personal communication, February 2011)

Undeniably, the profile of Jane and Finch, its reputation and the issues faced by its residents are more complex than what the lurid media stories communicate to a fearful, suspicious public and bewildered politicians. Residents' relationship to the area and its reputation include ambivalence, resistance and acceptance. Many residents seek to resist the representation of the area by media and others through activist work, forming community organizations, initiating projects, encouraging their children in education and challenging teachers and the school system. Some attempt to talk back to the media and others by saying this is a good place. After all, it is a place they call home where, despite the stigma and the different treatment they receive from people because they are from Jane and Finch, they come to recognize, in the words of one resident, "that nothing comes easy and that you have to work for whatever you are going to accomplish in life.... Yes, people might think of me as less because of where I live, but I would not submit to that" (*Sway* 2010: 42). It is the idea of home — or the safety and comfort of home — that prompted one young woman to say to the task force that was investigating community safety that she felt safe in the neighbourhood because of its strong sense of community — most people know each other and are willing to help each other.

While outsiders might wonder about residents' affection for the community, Jully Black's response to interview questions from Robert Ballantyne seems to provide the answer. The questions posed to Black were: "Tell me about your upbringing. What was it like being brought up in the tough area of Jane and Finch? Was it a nice community to grow up in, despite how the media portray it?" The questions critique media coverage even as they reinforce it. Black's response reflects a neighbourhood like any other, where today's children are unable to play freely and safely outside as was the case in earlier times.

> Of course, of course. The thing of an eight year old being able to run next door, to run up the street to grab something for your mom is over because of crime and all that stuff. But we were able to go to the mall by ourselves at young ages. We were able to create music and dance. The school is there, and the library is there. I remember back in the day — 'cause we didn't have computers — we'd go to the library to listen to music. It's still a community where there's a lot of growth going on. I'm proud of being from there, I lived there for eighteen years and it basically made me who I am today. (Ballantyne 2007)

Notes

1. This chapter was written with the assistance of Kulsoon Anwer. Also see her reflections in the concluding chapter.
2. The area known as Jane and Finch is bounded by Steeles Avenue to the north, Sheppard Avenue to the south, Highway 400 to the west, and Black Creek to the east.
3. This ambivalence likely has to do with the distance that the university, with its young middle-class student population, initially tried to keep from the community. In fact, while there have been very few incidents involving members of the community that have generated concern, these have caused York students to express fear of having to attend a university that is located in a "high-crime area" (Brown, Kennedy and Shin 2005).
4. This complex is the site of the 1999 drug-related shooting death of three-year-old girl who was killed in her father's car, in the complex's parking lot, by a bullet intended for her father, who was also wounded in the shooting. (Both killer and victims lived in the complex.) Sadly, this shooting was not an isolated incident. In many of the townhouse complexes in the area, residents can point out where someone was killed.
5. A popular adage or myth is that there are crocodiles in the Black Creek ravine that keep the residents from crossing onto university property.
6. In 2005, Chuckie Akenz (also known as Chuckie A.) of Jane and Finch, a

Vietnamese-Canadian rapper, released a controversial video for his single, "You Got Beef." The video was screened at the Vietnamese International Film Festival in California that year, but faced criticism for its glamorization of gang menace and apparent racism. The video reflects some of the racial tensions that exist in the area but its creators defend it as being about representation and self-esteem. Its director, Paul Nguyen, said the video is about "Vietnamese people finally taking a stand and working hard to insert themselves into the mainstream to be heard" (Han Nguyen 2005).

7. Hopefully, having students aged fifteen to eighteen from Jane and Finch working with the Toronto police through the Youth in Policing Initiative (YIPI) summer program, funded by the Ministry of Children and Youth Services and the Toronto Police Service Services Board, might result in young people from the area joining the police services in the future.

8. In the wake of these two holiday shootings, Toronto spoken word poet Dwayne Morgan, commenting on society's hierarchy of concern, wrote "I Wish My Friends Were White Girls": "Somehow, everything can be rationalized away, / As long as it stays over there, / But once it draws near, / We become the enemies in a culture of fear, / Where racism rears its head; / I wonder where the outcry of anger is / For the young Black men who lie dead" (Morgan 2005).

9. It is worth noting that, as in many suburban communities, Brampton is becoming racially diverse, with South Asians making up 37 percent of the population, Europeans or Whites, 34 percent, and Blacks, 16 percent. Nevertheless, the hegemonic Whiteness continues to frame those considered acceptable and assimilable residents.

10. It should be noted that many of Toronto's outer suburban areas are populated in part by people who initially lived in Jane and Finch: South Asians in Brampton, Mississauga, west of Toronto, and Markham, northeast of Toronto; Vietnamese, also in Brampton and Markham; and Italians in Vaughan, north-northwest of Toronto.

11. In June 2007, in an attempt to address the gang problem, police carried out raids of homes in the area starting at 6:30 a.m. Over 100 people were arrested for possessions of drugs, handguns, rifles and ammunition. Seventy-five were released (Marlow and Powell 2007). While some residents criticized the actions of the police, others agreed with the steps taken to rid the community of gangs — identified as the Crips and Bloodz — who were dividing the neighbourhood into north and south (Srikanthan 2007). According to a recent edition of the same newspaper, in 1998, among the estimated 180 "territorial-based crews, posses and gangs throughout the city, largely concentrated in poorer areas with public housing complexes" was Killaz, which operated in the Jane-Finch area (Powell 2010; see also Powell 2011).

Chapter 3

Schools, Educational Programs and Community

Urban schools, inner-city schools, high-needs schools; these are some of the euphemisms used to refer to schools located in low socio-economic or working-class communities such as Jane and Finch, typically serving populations of low-income, racial minority and immigrant students. Whatever the term used, it is often meant to identify, not only the geographic location of the school, but also the unstated or assumed relationship between that geography and the type of issues and concerns to be found among the students, parents and community members related to their social and cultural values, customs, expectations and aspirations. The fact is, schools in working-class ethnic minority neighbourhoods such as Jane and Finch, even though publicly funded, tend to be economically and socially disadvantaged. The schools lack the infrastructure as well as the necessary economic and political supports of those in middle-class neighbourhoods, which benefit from the formal and/or informal parent-driven fundraising activities that result in greater resources for students (Frenette 2007: 12). Furthermore, given the reputation of these schools, due in part to students' low level of performance, poor academic outcomes, high drop-out, suspension and expulsion rates, media representations and the number of special education classes for "at-risk" — or behavioural problem and academically failing — students, it is understandable that there would be a high burnout rate and despondency among teachers, as well as difficulty attracting teachers with the necessary commitment and expertise.

Nevertheless, schools in working-class communities remain vital in their role as socializing institutions that nurture the social and cultural capital that students bring to their education process. We know that students' educational outcomes are related to their socio-economic status (Contenta 1993; Dunne and Gazeley 2008; Fawcett and Scott 2007; Frenette 2007). The social circumstances and problems of working-class families, such as being unable to provide nutritious meals (sometimes children go without breakfast), and lack of time and knowledge of the school system to support their children's learning process, can and often do contribute to students' limited school participation, resulting in poor academic performance and achievement. While their middle-class counterparts enjoy home environments that are academically stimulating, with parents who have supportive contact with teachers, working-class students are more likely to have stressful home lives resulting from, among others, economic, social and cultural factors that are not conducive to learning.

Clearly, students from low-income backgrounds in a middle-class schooling system are at a disadvantage. Their disadvantage is further compounded if they are immigrant children or children of immigrants, and are of ethno-racial and linguistic minority backgrounds. This is because of their own or their parents' lack of familiarity with the school system and lack of English-speaking skills. While immigrant parents might have come from middle-class backgrounds and may have post-secondary education from their countries of origin (as tends to be the case for many of today's immigrants), once in Canada, most of them experience a downward socio-economic shift and hence do not enjoy the same class privilege as their Canadian counterparts. As Haan (2005) shows, today's immigrants experience low rates of employment or employment commensurate with their level of education, resulting in low income (compared to immigrants twenty years ago).[1] In such circumstances, Andrew Duffy (2003: 19) is correct in cautioning that

> there is reason to fear the emergence in Canada of an immigrant underclass. That fear becomes more vivid if the children of immigrants now living in poverty are not being equipped with the language skills and education they need to secure better jobs than their parents. Which is what brings me back to the classroom. Because it is here, I believe, that equity begins and where the growth of an underclass is forestalled.

While multiculturalism has been held up as proof of Canada's enlightened attitude toward accommodation of cultural diversity, in everyday life, in schools and other institutions, minority Canadians are not experiencing the acceptance of their differences as promised by Canada's official Multicultural Policy and Act and educational institutions' policies of multicultural education. According to Peter Li (2003: 8), "The contradiction of endorsing multiculturalism on the one hand and questioning immigrants' diversity on the other is resolved by adopting a rhetoric that upholds the ideological value of multiculturalism but dismisses the merit of cultural specificities." In light of this contradiction, then, multicultural education has been unable to provide both equality and equitable educational opportunities for all students. Students often encounter a multicultural discourse which portrays Canada as good, diverse and fair, without allowing space to accommodate their needs and desires in relation to their cultural experience (or background), especially as it is informed by race, colonialism and racism. As a consequence, immigrant and racial and ethnic minority students are often confronted with low teacher expectations, which can lead to low achievement and high drop-out rates; exceptions are those individuals constructed as model minority students (Cummins 2001; Gosine and James 2010).

Peter McLaren was probably one of the first teachers to publicly turn the city's attention to the schooling situation of Jane-Finch students with his book *Cries from the Corridor: The New Suburban Ghettos* (1981), which provided an intimate account of his years as a teacher inside the classroom and school in the late 1970s. McLaren, then a self-described ex-hippie, fresh out of university and flush with ideals, and now a noted academic in the area of urban and multicultural education, was widely criticized at the time by community members and educators alike for exposing the lives of the students. Nevertheless, his series of journal entries about the students' problems and his daily experiences with their socially unacceptable behaviours and educational disengagement provided a rich account of how the educational system (including some of the attitudes and expectations of his colleagues) were failing to meet the needs of the students. In fact, unlike media reporters' representations of the "corridor," McLaren demonstrated how the learning and teaching situation was directly related to the circumstances of his students' lives, and he called for teachers to change their understandings of the students.

Further, working with criticisms of this work (and being a critic of it himself), in subsequent years McLaren published portions of *Cries from the Corridor* in the highly acclaimed foundational text *Life in Schools: An Introduction to Critical Pedagogy in the Foundations of Education* (1998). This text advances the idea that the pedagogical approach to teaching, just like the curriculum content, must take into account the experiences of the students. The approach of critical pedagogy also holds that education is neither neutral nor apolitical, but is rooted in the dominant ideology evidenced through the history, politics and culture of the society. As such, the teachers' role, among others, must be to help students develop a critical understanding of how their individual circumstances, experiences and problems are related to the system of inequity and injustice in society (assuming that teachers have done the same for themselves). Schooling in such a context is not merely about having students "fit" into the existing system of meritocracy and standardized testing, but a terrain over which educators, like students and parents, constantly struggle over what is taught and learned, what is relevant to the students and what is legitimate knowledge — in essence, what they need to know to live, learn and appreciate their community and life within it. For low-income racialized students living in a "troubled" community, schooling has to be about appreciating the realities of their experiences, issues, concerns, interests and aspirations as they relate to the environment in which they live. It must also assist them in developing an awareness or consciousness of the economic, political, social and cultural differentiation of power so that they may take action if they so choose.

The Schools and Education Programs:
A Profile of Public School Students

At a minimum, there are nine public schools (five elementary, two middle and one high school) and five Catholic elementary and middle schools in Jane and Finch (an area of about three square miles or eight square kilometres, with an estimated total of 18,670 students between the ages of five and nineteen). I say at a minimum because there are at least seven schools[2] just outside of the boundary lines of Jane and Finch, and some children from the community do attend these. Hence, we can say that children and parents in the Jane-Finch area have access to more than twenty schools. Most of these schools were built in the 1960s and early 1970s, and one Catholic elementary school was built as early as 1952. The website of that school indicates that it

> was one of the first Catholic schools established in the south central area of North York. At the time it served a newly established development in a rural setting. During the late 50s, 60s, and 70s and well into the 80s the school met the needs of a predominantly Italian Canadian community. As of recent years it reflects a more diverse group in an established and older community.[3]

This statement is typical of many of the schools' websites that I examined to gain a sense of their perspectives, initiatives, innovations and trans-formations.[4]

The schools all identify that they serve a diverse population of students — a population that includes a diminishing number of Italians, most of whom attend the Catholic schools. As one public school indicates, its student population is "from Somalia, China, Vietnam, Cambodia, countries in West Africa, Costa Rica, Pakistan, Jamaica and several other Caribbean countries." It follows, therefore, that students and parents speak many languages other than English.[5] In fact, a few schools indicate that up to thirty different languages are spoken by students, and at least two schools indicate that "approximately sixty percent of [their] students speak a language other than English at home." However, the majority of the children are Canadian-born. This means that schools are not dealing with students whose language development takes place in an exclusively, for example, Cantonese-speaking environment. All of the Canadian-born students would have some exposure to English, no matter how limited. This has implications for the schools' English as a Second Language programs (Ippolito and Schecter 2008).

The schools all declare that they are committed to creating and facilitating an inclusive school community that is responsive to the needs of the students and respective of their cultural backgrounds.

> We believe that, *"All children can learn. Learning is the expectation."*

> We want every child to be successful and to be inspired to be a lifelong learner. We offer a wide range of learning opportunities that enrich and broaden our students' experiences in literacy and throughout the curriculum areas.... Our motto is... teachers make a difference.

> We provide a secure, caring and nurturing learning environment "to enable all students to reach high levels of achievement and to acquire the knowledge, skills and values they need to become responsible members of a democratic society."

> [The] mission statement confirms our commitment to empowering all students to be active participants in their learning and to building partnerships with the community, based on mutual respect. The school's motto: is "All Students Can Learn."[6]

The belief that all students can learn has compelled some schools to introduce "innovative learning opportunities that relate to their learning styles." Another school uses its arts programs to help students "develop self-confidence/discipline," thereby enabling them to become more focused and have their "cultural norms validated." But beyond the common refrain of educators that "all students can learn," what is presented for learning and the relevance of the learning material and teaching pedagogy to the students' experiences are absolutely vital to the learning process. In this regard, encouraging students to be "active participants" in their learning, as indicated in the quotation above, is indeed significant to the schooling process. However, for this to happen, students and their parents must be recognized as equal partners in deciding what is to be learned and its relevance to their aspirations and social, cultural and economic situation. It is fitting, as two schools did, to "subscribe to cultural proficiency and use parents' input to help shape curriculum." But what does that really mean, especially when teachers are largely guided by the Education, Quality and Accountability Office (EQAO), as one school noted, "to plan learning opportunities"? How does the curriculum premised on EQAO tests account for the social, cultural and economic circumstances of students? Would students in Jane and Finch receive an *equitable* education if their curriculum is the *same* as that of students in a more economically advantaged neighbourhood in Ontario?

Judging from their websites, many of the schools in the Jane-Finch area recognize that the schooling, educational, academic and recreation needs, interests and aspirations of students are interrelated to their social, cultural, economic, ethnic, gender, linguistic, religious and migrant backgrounds, as well as to their health.[7] In this regard, many schools have initiated programs and activities geared toward addressing the diverse needs of the students — from cultural to social support to nutritional needs — recognizing that productive learning-teaching relationships or students' attentive participation in class depend on successfully satisfying these needs. In many of the schools, we find language and heritage programs,[8] arts, recreation[9] or sports activities that take into account the cultural heritages of students; for example, the music and choir programs in some schools include violin, steelpan/band and drumming, and in the area of sports, cricket. Literacy and numeracy programs exist in a number of the schools; nevertheless, one school did admit that "our greatest academic challenge has been to address the literacy and numeracy skills of all of our students." But judging from the number of boys' programs with a literacy component — for instance, Boys' Book Club, Boys' Reading, and Boys2Men — it seems that there is particular concern for the literacy and, more generally, the academic skills of boys. According to the websites, other programs include special education classes for "special needs students" (e.g., children with "learning disabilities," "developmental delays," ADHD, "deaf and hard of hearing"), some of whom have access to social workers and child and youth workers. One school indicated that it has settlement workers that work with immigrant families, and another school speaks of having an "Islamic Prayer Group." Some schools also have nutrition programs through which students are provided breakfast, lunch and/or snacks.

At least two schools in the area are part of the Toronto District School Board's (TDSB) "cluster" of "Model Schools." The Model Schools for Inner Cities (MSIC) initiative is based on "five essential components":

> 1. innovative teaching and learning practices 2. support services to meet social, emotional and physical well being of students 3. school as the heart of the community 4. research, review and evaluation of students and programs and 5. commitment to share successful practice. Staff and students receive additional support in professional development events and resources which help the

students in their educational needs. (Yorkwoods Public School; see note 4)

As part of the MSIC program, Yorkwoods Public School was able to boast of being

> the only school in Ontario offering a unique reading software program called Fast ForWord that develops lasting changes within the brain. With its focus on listening accuracy, phonological awareness and structures, students using the program have shown significant improvement in memory, attention, processing rate and sequencing. Due to the daily use of the Fast ForWord products, Yorkwoods' students have reached high levels of completion and have shown great outcomes as a result.

A recurring theme on the schools' websites is the notion of providing a "safe environment" for students to learn. In other words, there is the recognition that students need to feel safe at school, and parents need to know that their children are safe. To this end, schools have initiated "safe arrival programs." In one case, parents are told that they "can contact the school 24 hours a day" and that they would be "contacted if the school does not hear" from them. Another school reports that "a no-violence tolerance policy is in effect both on and off school grounds. A strict discipline policy exists and is communicated in September by newsletter to all parents and students." Yet another school mentions that "the Toronto Police Department has been very supportive in helping us to maintain a safe environment." Knowing that all the area schools have put policies and programs in place to ensure safety[10] is indeed reassuring to parents, students and community members, especially in a community identified as having high rates of violence. However, schools should not only address the factors that contribute to the unsafe conditions in the school and community, but also the roots of those unsafe conditions — that is, the economic, social, political, cultural and educational conditions rooted in the inequities of the society. If indeed schools are committed to partnering with students — that is, having them be "active participants in their learning" — then, just as schools take up academic and athletic programs, so too schools must have conversations with students in their classes about things that they are experiencing in the community — things that might contribute to unsafe conditions.

On their websites, many of the area schools mention partnerships with parents, community social service agencies and educational institutions. This indicates a recognition among educators and administrators that parents must be partners in the schooling process of their children if schooling is to be meaningful to students. This idea was captured in the website statement of one school: "We know that children learn best when the school and parents work closely together to support each other and the learning of our students." Another school also noted that it is "deeply embedded in collaborating with our highly active parent community on numerous initiatives that enrich student learning. In addition, we work closely with our local community organizations on creating a safe and friendly environment for both our students and families." To this end, parents are able to volunteer in school activities, and some schools report having Parenting Centres that are housed inside the schools. In effect, a number of schools identify that they partner with local and city-wide community organizations to provide such things as mentorship (especially for boys), safety, service intervention, nutrition programs, fundraising and cultural activities, and parental supports. Through some of the partnerships with businesses (e.g., banks), schools have been able to meet and raise funds to support activities such as their nutrition programs.

One of the institutions with which many of the schools have a partnership is York University.[11] There is the eighteen-year Westview Partnership between the Faculty of Education and the Toronto District School Board. Through this partnership program, groups of teacher-candidates are placed in area schools and provided with the necessary academic supports to help them address the needs and interests of the students. Other activities include student visits to the university (starting as early as Grade 5), a summer program for Grade 8 students transitioning to high school, a summer science technology program (held in collaboration with Seneca College), student and parent conferences and a mentoring program for area students attending the university (WAY — Westview @York). There is also the Advance Credit Experience (ACE) for Grade 11 and 12 high-school students. Participants are placed at the university for one semester during which time they take one university course and do co-op work on campus in business and university program offices. It is thought that through this exposure to university programs participants will be motivated to attend university, and those who choose to attend York are eligible for a scholarship provided by the York Faculty Association. Another partnership program is with a college at the university. The website of the elementary school involved in this partnership describes it as "a unique learning partnership with Vanier College, York University. More than 400 university students are involved with Literacy, Mentorship, French and a Play in Peace Program."

From the information on the schools' websites we can say that, in most cases, there is implicit and explicit recognition among school personnel of the significance of giving attention to the cultural context of the students, particularly to their cultural background in terms of being immigrants or having immigrant parents. In this regard, we see attempts to address language and related literacy needs and skills, and consent to religious practices. There was some mention of services for students with various "disabilities" and those "experiencing emotional or behavioural difficulties" (this group of students is said to have access to a psychologist). But what about the programs designed to deal with the emotional and mental health of students? Surely, in some cases, things perceived to be "learning disabilities" or "developmental delays" and other such "special needs" might have their roots in the psychological condition of a student. Hence, to effectively address the needs of students or the concerns of teachers and parents about the behaviour of students requires that educators give attention to or become "literate" in the mental and emotional health of students, just as they do with the students' literacy skills.

Much is said about constructing curriculum and engaging in school activities that acknowledge the "culture" of students and their parents — in fact, parents and other community members are invited to participate in school activities that would give exposure to their "ethnic culture." While this might be a plausible move, insofar as it represents teachers' efforts to move beyond the dominant ethno-racial discourse of the curriculum that operates to alienate, marginalize and racialize working-class and ethno-racial minority students (Dei et al. 2000), it should always be borne in mind that the students in our classrooms are Canadians and so are their values, behaviours, customs and artifacts (James 2010a). However, these attributes are also informed by the realities of the community in which they live, play and learn. Hence, the understanding of the cultures of the students must necessarily take that reality into account. So beyond addressing the "cultures" of the students, there is little or no evidence of how schools help students make sense of their community — in other words, what is absent is information about social class, poverty or the material circumstances that contribute to the disparities in economic resources. This is a notable absence, but perhaps such information is beyond the scope of the websites. Information about the literacy test scores of the schools is also absent — something that could be a selling point.

However, there is a video on one elementary school's website in which some school children articulate on "What is poverty to a kid?" (Risling and Simmie 2008). What is interesting is their thinking of poverty in relation to homeless people. As they talked about people having to "go to food banks to get food," and the need for homeless people to be housed, helped, given "nice clothes" and cared for, there is a hint that somehow these young people have experience at some level with poverty. Take for instance the words of one boy: "What if you lose your job somehow, and can't get it back because you have no other skills? We have to care for other people too; 'cause they have difficult lives. They didn't go to school; how are they going to get a job? We need to give them a chance in jobs because they need it, and they need to get money so that they could feed their children themselves." Insofar as poverty is a reality in the community, it is something that should be discussed in relation to the students' lives and not something to be avoided. In other words, teachers have a role to play, through curriculum materials, pedagogical approaches and co-curricular activities in helping students to become critical readers and interpreters of the world around them, whose messages or images (especially as conveyed by media) of their community contradict their own.

Given the expectations and challenges that teachers are likely to confront in a community such as Jane and Finch, it is worth exploring how they understand and carry out their role and responsibility as teachers. What are some of the issues teachers face in their work with students in the area? What does it take for them to respond to the needs, issues and concerns of the students and parents with whom they work? What does it take to make the schooling and educational program of students relevant to their needs and interests? Does a diverse staff population that seems to physically reflect the diverse population of the students help? Is it enough? Does being a racial minority teacher make a difference in the relationships that teachers are able to develop with the students and hence make for more productive and/or successful schooling? These are some of the questions I posited to a group of public school teachers working in a racially mixed (majority racial minority students) school in the area. What follows are the observations, ideas and perceptions of the eighteen (twelve female, six male) teachers. Eight of the teachers were of African-Caribbean origin, two were South Asian, and the others, European.

Teachers' Perceptions and Concerns about Students

Before proceeding, it is worth pointing out that some teachers had reservations about sharing their experiences and perceptions of teaching in the area because they did not wish to import or confirm media images of the community and the students. In other words, they did not wish to engage in stereotyping. This allowed us to determine that, to work effectively with any group in whatever situation, we have to identify the group, name the issues and come to an understanding of the context in relation to the social, economic, cultural and political realities. That said, the teachers and I talked about having to understand the issues of the students in relation to the conditions of the area, just as we would at another school and in another area of the city. Education, we agreed, always has to be approached in the context of the students' lives.

The teachers acknowledged that the community's stigmatization, poverty, and the ethnic, racial and religious diversity of the students made teaching there a particularly demanding task. As such, they understood — theoretically at least — that they had to pay attention to the conditions under which the students live and, in turn, develop strategies through which they could effectively engage students and their parents in the schooling and educational process. As one teacher put it, "We have to be realistic. We have to take into account, not only their educational life, but also their family life." As well, "It is not just what happens in school," said another teacher. "Students bring their expectations from home, and the messages they get from the society" — a society in which they are "bombarded with things that they cannot manage." The teachers noted that there was a lack of motivation and sense of resignation among the students that was voiced in statements such as "I don't want to do it" and "I don't care if I pass." And they referred to cases in which students failed to complete homework assignments. Students, some teachers felt, "seem to settle for the lowest," believing that they would be able to get a job with whatever credits they managed to accumulate in high school. There was the recognition that students' tendency to question the relevance of education and the value of math to their future played a role in the manner in which they "checked out" of the learning process; probably, as the teachers assumed, "to check back in when they find education relevant." Teachers observed that there were gender differences in the ambitions and the ways in which students applied themselves to their academic work — boys were less attentive and more often subject to disciplinary action.

The teachers identified a number of personal issues as contributing to the students' approach to their education and their educational problems. Significant among the issues is the problem of anger. "I see a lot of anger," said one teacher. "I see it in a variety of students. I do not know where it comes from." Among the other interrelated problems mentioned were identity, aspirations and ambitions, punctuality, lack of role models, peer group relations and discipline. It was ascertained that identity was a problem for students. Referring to racial minority students, particularly Black students, the teachers contended that "children do not know who they are; they have no sense of belonging." This lack of a strong sense of identity was thought to undermine the students' self-confidence, which simultaneously contributed to their feelings of alienation and their attempts to protect themselves by "covering up" or hiding their fear of taking risks. It was also surmised that the students' poor academic performance, lateness and absences from school were part of their protective strategy — something that the teachers appeared not to know how to address. Nevertheless, the teachers seemed to accept that the students' actions signalled that they needed to see purpose in their education in order for them to establish a stake in it. Furthermore, as the teachers would later disclose, students' home responsibilities, such as babysitting their younger siblings and taking care of home tasks while their parents — in many cases, single mothers — were at work, sometimes required them to stay home from school or were the reason for them arriving late at school (see also James and Taylor 2010).

The major theme in my conversation with the teachers was the need for role models who would provide guidance and support to students, especially male role models, given the absence of fathers. As one teacher said, "The students have strong mothers but no fathers; they lack male role models at home. Most of the time it is their mother they see; male teachers in the school helps." Another teacher said that "male teachers are important; [students] have lots of females in their lives.... Male teachers help to provide structure and framework" (see Martino and Rezai-Rashti 2010 for a critical reflection of this point). For many teachers, this absence of what they regard as an important socializing parent at home had a great deal to do with the students' attitudes and behaviours in school. Attempts to instil a sense of decorum, social and academic discipline, and responsibility were met with resistance. One form of resistance was in their "ways of dressing," even (or especially) at a school in which a uniform was required. It was observed that "school uniforms make no difference.... This might be great for administration; but school performance does not change whether they are wearing uniforms or not." Males were found to be less compliant than females.

The teachers hypothesized that, at home, students are accustomed to authoritarian approaches to discipline — something they associated with the cultural backgrounds of the students' parents (Caribbean was identified as one such background). Hence, according to the teachers, giving choices to students was contrary to how students expected to be treated. On this point, one teacher questioned: "Do the school and teachers have to follow the same disciplinary practices as the students get at home?" The sentiment of most teachers in response to this question was that doing so would be difficult within the context of a culturally diverse student population with different cultural norms, values and academic interests. Further complicating the problem of discipline is what one teacher referred to as the students' undeveloped sense of responsibility. "Students have an underdeveloped concept of rights," she said. "It is not balanced with their sense of responsibility." Teachers reasoned that there cannot be uniformity across the school since teachers have different expectations and levels of tolerance — differences that students exploit. These affect the kinds of discipline that a teacher administers and ultimately the tone of the school.

As in many of today's multicultural school environments, these teachers worked at a school where there are posters welcoming students, parents and visitors in different languages, posters with quotations by famous racialized people and of pictures or images that reflect the ethno-racial diversity of the students. There were also cultural artifacts and symbols (e.g., flags) representing the cultural origins of the students or their families. When asked how effective these cultural and ethno-racial representations were in helping students and parents to feel more welcomed and less alienated in the school, the teachers were ambivalent, if not doubtful. They questioned the extent to which students or parents really understood the message of inclusivity and equity that was being communicated. Several teachers felt that a consequence of this attempt to help students feel empowered is the advantage that some racial minority students occasionally took of situations in which they experienced problems with teachers, specifically White teachers. On such occasions the students would call attention to race and accuse the teacher of racism. It was said that having such experiences made teachers "feel vulnerable" — something that teachers struggle to deal with.

In telling of how they have attempted to deal (or have dealt) with students' "lack of motivation," academic performance, perceptions of limited possibilities and discipline problems, and their own vulnerability when they are "pushed" by students, the teachers' responses reveal that they look less at themselves but more at the students and what they regard as their manifest commitment to teaching them:

> "We're fighting to teach them."

> "It is hard to hear some students say that university is not for them."

> "Some students are not ready for learning and promoting[12] them is a disservice."

> "Give students a choice [of educational routes they can take]."

> "It is absolutely important to get parents involved [in all school activities]."

> "We need to provide another setting."

The teachers also reported that they would ask students what they expected of themselves and for their future, and would try to convince students that "they can turn their lives around." The teachers acknowledged that education is not value-free and that their role as teachers is to prepare students to be functional members of society. As one teacher said: "I want them to realize that this is a game and they have to learn how to play it."

In terms of pedagogy, a number of the teachers indicated that they use stories from assigned reading materials to communicate the message of what is possible through education. But, they also questioned the extent to which "motivational stories or success stories really work." And they accepted that, in many cases, they are working with "texts that do not represent who is in the school." To counteract this situation, some teachers used supplementary texts with what they considered to be "relevant" materials. When asked about using educational texts written in the languages of the students, one teacher cautioned, "We cannot confuse them, thus endangering their development in the necessary language skills and abilities. This is not good for the students. It will contribute to mixed expectations." Another teacher offered a contrary view:

> Engaging students in their language helps to validate where they're coming from, and where they are going. We have to make creative use of their culture, for example, rap. We have to respect where they are coming from, then present other things. Do not suggest that one is better than another. Start with where they are at. Validate their language [i.e., dialect].

However, there was a caution against "diluting the [educational] program because we accept equality, and [are] working with the idea that everyone has to be successful." Here one teacher questioned the merits of inclusivity and equity — "Equity at what cost?" — if the educational program and, correspondingly, educators' expectations are "diluted" because "we all have to feel good."

Generally, the teachers saw their mission as helping "students to be motivated to succeed" and to work against the system's practice of promoting students (see comment above, where one teacher referred to this as a "disservice") regardless of the work they produce. Many of the teachers felt that they "have given their all" to working with students and parents in ways that would result in the students' educational productivity and school engagement. But there are difficulties, teachers admit, to realizing these goals. For one, there is the lack of involvement by parents in the schooling process of their children. Some teachers reported trying to contact parents, but this did not always yield the results they wished. While in most cases communication with parents was often difficult, when teachers did get a chance to talk with them, the parents committed to working to "change things." But according to the teachers, "that only lasts for about two days." Another difficulty has to do with school administration: specifically, the expectations and pressure that administrators placed on teachers — which the teachers concede have been passed on from the Board — around test scores.[13] It was suggested that the importance placed on test scores caused administrators to want teachers to focus, sometimes almost exclusively, on drilling students on the tests. But as one person questioned, "At whose expense?" The teachers saw the expectations and pressures they "have to endure" as contributing to high staff turnover in the school.

Returning to their discourse of role models, I asked: Does a diverse staff population that is reflective of racial diversity of the students help? There was agreement among many of the teachers that staff diversity helped, but, with emphasis, some said "to an extent." According to one teacher, "Staff diversity helps, but it is secondary." Another added: "It is not enough, but it might help to inform." With reference to how Black students might relate to Black teachers, one Black teacher submitted: "Black students identify us Black teachers with the establishment. They don't think that we inhabit their world; we can't relate to them. They perceive us to be maintaining the system." Nevertheless, as one Black teacher put it, "We can better identify with the issues of the students"; and another added: "Our presence says a lot to the students." A common sentiment among many of the Black teachers was that it is possible for them to "affect the lives of the students we teach" and address their "low expectations." And in the words of one teacher, students "need teachers who understand their backgrounds."

For the most part, teachers were quite conversant with the many issues with which they struggled in teaching students in the area, and they were not only able to demonstrate an understanding of the issues, but had suggestions for what should be done. Some teachers appreciated the gaps in their thinking and the number of concerns yet to be addressed. One concern was that students were not completing their homework. What Pease-Alvarez, Angelillo and Chavajay (2005: 134) have to say about homework is instructive. They argue that, for many parents, homework provides their children with the chance to practise what they have learned in school, and provides them "with opportunities to connect with their children's learning." However, the difficulty with homework is that it some-times burdens parents with extra work, exposes the limitation of parents' education, obligates parents to create a particular home environment for learning and takes children away from their home responsibilities. Given the dearth of research about homework in Canada, it would be useful to examine students' engagement and accomplishments regarding home-work (including particular types of homework) in relation to family and cultural resources and contexts. Indeed, studies have shown that children's homework activities with others involve complex and dynamic cultural teaching and learning processes; hence it is necessary to take into account the social and cultural contexts that enable or impede children's successful engagements in homework activities with others (Pease-Alvarez, Angelillo and Chavajay 2005; see also Mandell and Sweet 2004).

Another major concern of the teachers was how to get parents involved in their children's lives and school activities. In their article "Engaging the Discourse of Diversity: Educators' Frameworks for Working with Linguistic and Cultural Difference," Pacini-Ketchabaw and Schecter (2002: 46) offer a helpful perspective based on their work at a school in the Greater Toronto Area. They argue for teachers to incorporate the diverse cultural experiences of students into their teaching and learning and not see students' "difference as deficit." Those teachers who saw students' "difference as deficit" tended to believe that the "bilingual abilities of students represent both a barrier to their ability to learn and an inconvenience for their teachers." As a consequence, it was expected that parents would do things in ways that would "facilitate the school's agenda." The authors tell of teachers with whom they worked who would acknowledge the cultural, linguistic and racial diversity of their student population but saw their role as socializing parents "to the agenda of mainstream schooling and to familiarize them with the protocols that professional educators endorsed and used."

Pacini-Ketchabaw and Schecter (2002) also observed that teachers who familiarized themselves with students' backgrounds in an effort to be more responsive to their differing learning needs were not as successful as might be expected in the teaching and learning process. A middle-school teacher offers a probable reason for this:

> It is quite difficult for teachers to change their understanding of home cultures as deficient, rather than just different. It requires a significant mental shift that takes considerable maintenance and vigilance. Although I embrace the framework of "Diversity as Curriculum" as helping to build better home-school relations — among other things, I find it difficult, particularly at the high-school level where we are preparing students for post-secondary worlds that are completely disjointed from their home cultures, to incorporate it into my teaching practice in any significant way. Perhaps, what I mean to say is that even if a teacher does not view the home culture as deficient, it is hard to progress to viewing it as a resource. I question whether it is possible to do the former without the latter. (Anne (pseudonym), Personal communication, December 2005)

What is conveyed in the teachers' comments is that they need help to develop strategies in how to work differently with their students and parents. According to one teacher, "We need a program that the students can relate to. They cannot relate to what we are presenting."

Obviously, this call for information and strategies on how to work differently means that teachers wish to go beyond their good intentions. Indeed, good intentions are not enough, for while these intentions have helped teachers to achieve a level of social and cultural consciousness and sensitivity related to equity and inclusivity in the educational process, by their own admission they had yet to develop an educational program and curriculum by which they are able to confidently respond to the needs, interest and circumstances of their students. A case in point is the teachers' call to students to think about the importance of education to their future, particularly in terms of attaining a post-secondary education and concomitantly a successful career. While such encouragement might be useful, engaging students about their future might be futile since it is impossible for them to envision that constructed future in the context of their present circumstances — circumstances teachers often never address or even acknowledge. The fact is, teachers have to deal with the now: start with how students experience and understand their community, their place within it, their immediate situation and in turn their possibilities — only then are students more likely to engage with their schooling. It is conceivable that schooling will remain irrelevant to students if teachers and, in particular, their assigned role models and mentors (we will return to this in Chapter 5) insist that the community they understand as home is a transient place— a space in which they have no roots — and can only prepare them for a life outside of it.

It is common practice for teachers to blame parents and for parents to blame teachers for the failure of students, but as Patriakou et al. (2005: 23) point out, "In fact, the fault actually lies with the interface between home and school." Therefore, it should be an ongoing practice for teachers to give attention to the role that the interactions between community, parents and families, and school play in responding to problems, or in helping students meet the demands of schooling. And in cases where social, cultural and other differences seem to undermine the collaborative efforts of schools, parents and community members, school-community partnerships can help toward developing innovative programs that are responsive to the cultural differences or barriers faced by students and parents.

The issues and problems that educators encounter in today's schools point to the need to give concerted attention to how students' experiences outside of school affect their educational performance. Attention must also be given to how communities and parents and families — with all their variations — have acted and might continue to act as resources to schools in ways that are consistent with the inclusive, democratic and egalitarian aims of education and schooling. University partnerships with schools, school boards, community organizations and ministries of education could certainly help, not only to carry out crucial research, but also to facilitate the kinds of programs necessary to build a community-centred and politically conscious partnership — something that will also inform teacher education programs. In fact, this suggestion came from the teachers with whom I spoke. Specifically, York University needs to do "more for the community," and to this end, work with the school board and schools to construct programs that are responsive to the needs of students, educators, parents, administrators and communities.

Conclusion

The markers of school success, such as school participation, level of standardized performance, academic achievements, graduation and university attendance, indicate that students in the Jane-Finch area continue to perform very poorly. While many administrators, teachers and other resource educators are doing their best to reverse the poor performance of students, there is still much work to be done. Initiatives such as the Model Schools for Inner Cities programs (in which low-income area schools receive extra educational and financial supports) and other school-board-university partnership activities are not having the expected impact. This may have to do with the fact that students are not feeling the same sense of urgency as their teachers and parents in relation to applying themselves to their studies. But why should they, when educators and others charged with educating them have yet to fully and effectively engage them in an educational program that is responsive to their needs, interests and aspirations? Indeed, students need educational programs rooted in their community and familial experiences and culture. They also need to see the beneficial relationship between their current education and their future in society. As well, teachers need to appreciate students' questions pertaining to where their education will take them — a question that is sometimes mired in doubt, ambivalence and resignation, given their experiences with marginalization. While resignation in the face of complex and persistent problems is inevitable to some degree, it does not, however, make resignation acceptable.

In their report *The Strength and Challenges of Community Organizing as an Educational Reform Strategy*, Renée and McAlister (2011: 2) argue that collaboration and partnership between youth, parents, community members and educators working within institutions such as schools and universities can alter resource and power inequities that produce failing schools in marginalized communities. Such collective actions can create "accountable, equitable, high-quality schools for all students by challenging the patterns of inequity that are built into the rules [or policies] and laws that guide the school." They argue that the assessment measures, such as standardized tests, that are used to evaluate student learning operate more to justify the judgment — including the rewards and sanctions — that we pass on students in schools, especially those that "fail to show growth according to those assessments." According to the authors,

> This approach focuses on holding students accountable for learning and teachers for teaching, but does not hold policy-makers accountable for providing the resources or conditions needed for students to learn. Community organizing, in contrast, focuses on the accountability of policy-makers and school leaders to students, parents, and the community. From this standpoint, low test scores are seen not as a failure of a single student, teacher, or principal, or the unfortunate consequence of a complex social factors, but as proof that the education system is failing to provide all young people with all of the opportunities, resources, and supports they need to become educated citizens. (2)

Respecting and acknowledging the agency of students, parents and community members through partnerships with schools can certainly enrich the teaching and learning experiences of students. What is relevant here is the need for educators to constantly re-examine and revise how they construct students as learners and the expectations that they hold of them. In such a context, value and emphasis must be placed on family and community engagement. In doing so, educators must reframe how Jane and Finch is conceptualized and mediated, not as a space and place from which individuals are expected to move, but rather as a community that serves and will continue to serve as home to a significant number of Canadian children and families.

Notes

1. Haan (2005: 2193) shows that while immigrants from twenty-five to thirty-four years of age earned approximately $4,300 less than Canadian-born workers in 1981, that disparity grew to $6,000 by 2001.
2. That number refers to four public and one Catholic elementary school, one public middle school, and one public and one Catholic high school.
3. St. Charles Borromeo at <tcdsb.org/schools/stcharles.asp>
4. Public schools: Driftwood Public School at <tdsb.on.ca/schools/index.asp?schno=3100>; Firgrove Public School at <tdsb.on.ca/firgrove/>; Gosford Public School at <tdsb.on.ca/SchoolWeb/_site/viewitem.asp?siteid=10004&pageid=6411&menuid=7336>; Stanley Public School at <tdsb.on.ca/schools/index.asp?schno=3260>; Topcliff Public School at <tdsb.on.ca/schools/index.asp?schno=3267>; Yorkwoods Public School at <tdsb.on.ca/schools/

index.asp?schno=3296>; Brookview Middle School at <tdsb.on.ca/schools/
index.asp?schno=3180>; Oakdale Middle School at <tdsb.on.ca/schools/index.
asp?schno=3209>; Westview Centennial Secondary School at. Catholic Schools: Blessed Margherita of Citta Castello Separate
School at <tcdsb.org/schools/blessedmargherita.asp>; St. Augustine Catholic
School at <tcdsb.org/schools/staugustine.asp>; St. Charles Garnier Separate
School at <tcdsb.org/schools/stcharlesgarnier.asp>; St. Francis De Sales School
at <tcdsb.org/schools/stfrancisdesales.asp>; St. Jane Frances Parish at <tcdsb.
org/schools/stjanefrances.asp>.

5. One school reveals that their students come from as many as twenty-five different countries. Another school noted that "about 30% of our students are of
Caribbean heritage, about 30% are of Southeast Asian descent, and about 15% of
our students are of South American descent. The remaining 25% of the students
come from almost every other part of the globe... [and] 90% of our students or
their parents have immigrated to Canada."

6. Quotations are from the following websites: Shoreham Public School at <tdsb.
on.ca/profiles/3247.pdf> and <tdsb.on.ca/Schools/index.asp?schno=3247>;
Driftwood Public School at <tdsb.on.ca/schools/index.asp?schno=3100>; Firgrove
Public School at <schools.tdsb.on.ca/firgrove/>; Brookview Middle School at
<tdsb.on.ca/profiles/3180.pdf>.

7. One school indicated that students are given hearing and vision screening, and
LensCrafters provides free pairs of glasses for students who need them.

8. These programs include English as a Second Language (ESL), International
Languages, African Heritage (History) Month, Asian Heritage Month and what
one school terms "Diversity Celebrations."

9. Interestingly, one MSIC school revealed that through the initiative "students [have]
the opportunity to participate in activities such as ballroom dancing."

10. It should be noted that the wearing of uniforms is considered part of the safety
routine since students who attend the school are more visible to school administrators and staff, differentiating them from visitors and intruders.

11. It is worth mentioning that, in part, many of these partnership programs emerge
from community members' demands — heard at meetings held with members
of the university — that university members do more for the community and not
use the community for their own selfish interests. One of these meetings was
held in November 2002.

12. This is commonly referred to as "transferring" students, meaning that they did
not pass or gain the necessary credits to be "promoted" to the next grade.

13. In a *Globe and Mail* article (Friesen 2006: A1) that compared three middle schools
that serve students in the Jane-Finch area, the reporter, referencing students'
performance on tests, observed that students attending the middle school located
outside of the Jane-Finch border performed much better. He acknowledged that,
on the TDSB's Learning Opportunities Index that rated schools according to need,
the schools within the community were assessed as far more needy. Nonetheless,
the school's Director of Special Programs contended that students at the school
outside of Jane and Finch were not very different from those in the Jane-Finch
area, and attributed the better performance to the school's comprehensive curriculum and teachers who commit a lot of extra hours to helping their students
succeed.

Chapter 4

Relying on Education
Community, Schooling and Educational Ambitions

In spite of the poverty, marginalization and an education system that has yet to come to grips with how best to effectively respond to their needs, many of the youth in Jane and Finch nonetheless remain resilient. They hold onto a hope that through education they will be able to realize their career aspirations, which they construct in relation to the needs of their community. The youth's hope seems to emerge from their understanding of their individual and community situation, as well as from knowing that it is through individual and collective action that the necessary changes in people's perceptions and actions toward their community will occur. So, framed by their sense of hope — a commitment to critically engage in a process of liberation from oppression (Friere 1994) and see beyond their immediate despair (Daloz et al. 1996) — the youth seem to willingly invest their time and energy into working on ways to better, not only their own lives, but those of other individuals and families, and thereby change the image of their community.

My experiences with the aspirations of the youth, particularly those whom I meet at the neighbourhood schools and with whom I work in the university, have motivated the research I have conducted in the area since 1994. Many of these experiences were made possible through the Westview Partnership that the Faculty of Education at York University has had with the Toronto District School Board since 1991.[1] The partnership seeks to enrich the schooling experience through programs designed to meet the needs, interests and expectations of students, teachers, parents, administrators and teacher candidates. Among the many programs offered through the partnership is the University Path Program, with activities geared toward helping students — even those in middle school — to seriously consider university as an option after high school. The program operates on the premise that "students' failures are due not merely to their individual efforts, social situation, or cultures but also to educational and social contexts and structural barriers that limit their capacity to imagine and pursue certain possibilities after high school" (James and Haig-Brown 2001: 231; see also College Student Alliance et al. 2011). Information about university requirements and scholarship opportunities and support with the application process are provided to students. At one time, students were able to participate in a summer internship with a science professor. A number of students who participated in the University Path Program made it to York University, with some of them becoming teachers.[2]

In this chapter, I refer to a number of studies that I have conducted with students in the Jane and Finch community. In one of my first studies, I examined the experiences, perceptions and aspirations of twelve university students who were part of the University Path Program during high school (James 2005; James and Haig-Brown 2001). Rebecca, Nancy, Akaos, Sumita, Nguyen, Catherine, Vivian and others[3] participated in this research and were interviewed individually during their second year of university. They were between the ages of twenty-two and twenty-six, and all had graduated from high school with averages in the 70s and 80s. Four of the participants were born in Canada. The others were born in Vietnam, Cambodia, India, Sri Lanka, Jamaica, Ghana and New York. At least two of those born in Canada had immigrant parents from the Caribbean, including Guyana. The study revealed varied understandings and constructions of the spatial area in which they lived, and how career aspirations (predominantly in human services professions) were structured as a response to their perception of the needs of the "community" (James and Haig-Brown 2001).

I also refer to the findings from a study I conducted with a group of twenty second-generation and generation-and-a-half students between the ages of eighteen and twenty-five who lived in Metropolitan Toronto (James 2005). Two of these participants (Jamaican-born Conrad and Canadian-born Kendra) were from the Jane and Finch area and had attended the local high school and then York University on scholarship. In the individual interviews that were part of the larger study, I sought to find out

> how the raced experiences of participants informed their construction, understanding and articulation of their identity as Canadians and concomitantly their perceptions of their educational and career opportunities and possibilities.... [and] how their experiences traversing their social, educational, cultural, economic, and occupational structures of the Toronto society [were] mediated by the social and cultural references and expectation of their immigrant parents and the "Caribbean community" in Toronto. (James 2010b: 123)

A third study to which I refer is one we conducted with Toronto youth between the ages of fifteen and twenty-five who had had some encounters with the justice system because of the disciplinary actions taken by their schools. Through focus group interviews with about forty, mostly male, youth,[4] many of them African Canadians, the research team of lawyers, educators and youth sought to learn "about the youth's views of the legal system based on their experiences with police, lawyers and judges (and in a few cases, correctional officers working in prisons)" (James and Taylor 2010: 125). The study included youth from Jane and Finch and other disadvantaged urban neighbourhoods in the northwest of Toronto. Further, while the study did not set out to investigate the educational and occupational aspirations of these youth, as they talked about their schooling they revealed how much they were aware of the significance of education to their lives. These students repeatedly related their experiences in school and with the justice system to a larger socio-political struggle, meaning that they were not offered the education they needed or access to what they considered to be "justice" in education. They believed that they were unfairly judged, not for who they are, but by the colour of their skin, where they live and how they dressed. They saw their identification as "at-risk" students as an "excuse" for teachers to maintain their prejudgements and behave in a duplicitous manner toward them. And even when it did appear that teachers were being compassionate and caring, the students remained unconvinced and suspicious of them because they knew too well of the staff room gossip that further stigmatizes and burdens. Nonetheless, still convinced that there is no alternative to school, they went on to point out that teachers need to get to "know" about their lives and about their "struggles" inside and outside of school if they are to fully engage them as students in the teaching and learning process (James and Taylor 2010).

Embedded in the narratives of the youth who participated in the studies I have conducted and those with whom I have worked at the university is the idea that they must get a "good education." They see such education not only as the means by which they will be able to attain their occupational or career goals, but also as a way to counteract the stereotypes or stigmatization of themselves and the community in which they have grown up and live. In essence, the studies establish that community played a significant role in shaping the ways the youth assessed their schooling (high school and university) and their career aspirations. Their aspirations were constructed in relation to their reading of their community's needs and issues, their reactions to the prevailing outsiders' views of the community and their belief that through their education, and eventually the jobs they come to occupy, the stigma that has plagued them and their community over the years will be removed. Education, then, for many of the young people was not something in which they engaged simply to "get a job." Nor was it limited to the dictates of the North American trajectory of going to school, getting a job, "settling down" (i.e., marrying), buying a house and retiring. Rather, education generally, and higher education in particular, was conceived of as a means of acquiring the necessary skills to take advantage of opportunities and exercise their agency in order to contribute to a positive view of their community — both the geographic and ethno-racial community with which they identify.

Clearly, the young people of Jane and Finch were not unusual in seeing education as essential to whatever they might be able to accomplish for themselves and their community (James and Taylor 2008; López 2002; Schecter and Bailey 2002; Wood 2011). But there are questions that should be considered with regard to their investment in education. Why do they think that things will be different because of their efforts, when, like their friends, family and community members, they are receiving their education in an institutional context that has created the situation in which they find themselves? Why do they think that a system that has helped to shape and maintain the structures that marginalize them will provide space for them and their peers to learn on the basis of their needs, interests and aspirations? Why do they think that educators and others within the education system will be receptive to their input into how to make education relevant and responsive to their needs, interest and expectations? Why do they continue to bank on education — its principles, ideals and promises — to address and change their situation and that of their community? What sustains their perception of education as meritocratic, equitable, emancipatory and transformative?

In the absence of other resources, such as adequate finances and a network of significant others to assist the youth to gain access to opportunities, education remains the one most accessible[5] — hence, the optimism and hope that they place in education. Therefore, the straightforward answer to the above questions would be that there are no other alternatives. As a consequence, they come to rely on their knowledge, abilities and skills as nurtured by their respective families and communities to meet the challenges that they must face to realize their ambitions. Further, this sense of hope and optimism is related to the "community cultural wealth" upon which the young people draw. According to Yosso (2005: 77), community cultural wealth is the "array of knowledge, skills, abilities and contacts" that members of a community possess and utilize in their bid to survive and resist their marginalization, racialization and/or oppression. Yosso identifies six forms of community cultural wealth: aspirational, familial, social, linguistic, navigational and resistant capital. She writes:

> These forms of capital are not mutually exclusive or static, but rather are dynamic processes that build on one another as part of community cultural wealth. For example, aspirational capital is the ability to hold on to hope in the face of structured

inequality and often without the means to make such dreams a reality. Yet, aspirations are developed within social and familial contexts, often through linguistic storytelling and advice… that offer specific navigational goals and challenge (resist) oppressive conditions. (77)

The role, significance and impact that community plays in the lives of marginalized youth varies in relation to, among other factors, where they live, their ethno-racial identity, their length of time in Canada (or generation), the message they receive from significant others about their community and their proximity to post-secondary opportunities. This became clear in my studies of Black post-secondary students living in the Greater Toronto Area and those living specifically in the Jane-Finch community. A comparison of their experiences, interests and aspirations reveals that both groups had high educational and career aspirations that were influenced by their desire to challenge or contradict the widely held perception of themselves as low achievers because of their race, to resist their racialization and marginalization and to use their careers in service to their community. They aspired to become teachers, social workers, lawyers, politicians and business people, and all of them indicated that they expected these careers to qualify and provide them with the necessary resources to "give back" to their communities, thereby enhancing their own occupational opportunities, as well as those of younger disenfranchised members.

However, there were differences in the way the two groups of youth talked about their communities. The Toronto-wide, second-generation Black youth[6] defined "community" in racial terms — Blackness, with little or no reference to regional or national differences. And their idea of "giving back" to their community was not about working in a community defined by geography, but one defined simply in terms of Blackness. In this regard, recognizing that the community of Black people can be defined only by network and not geography, these youth talked in terms of the influence they wish or expect to have on the larger societal structures through the occupations to which they aspired or eventually attained. An example of this anticipated influence and their group affinity is found in Kisha's comments regarding her plans to enter a master's program in education at a Toronto university. She explained: "I'd like to start some programs in my area with Black youth and maybe go back to my high school and do some teaching…. I'd like to do some programming in the community." Roxanne, on the other hand, a teacher-candidate at the time of the interview, said that she pursued kinesiology in university, not merely to become a physical education teacher — something she felt was "expected" of her because she is Black and was an athlete — but because of her interest in "the science side of sports and I thought about majoring in science.... I thought about doing math or something where you didn't see a lot of black people, just for that reason" (James 2005: 220).

On the other hand, the Jane-Finch youth — of Caribbean and African origin[7] — talked of their community first in terms of geography, with fixed physical coordinates or boundaries, and second in terms of ethno-racial identities. Like their South and East Asian counterparts, the Black youth were driven by their desire to dispel the unfair negative stereotypes of the Jane-Finch community and "give back" to their respective ethno-racial group members residing there. However, even as they talked about giving back to their community, many also expressed a desire to eventually leave it — and leave behind the negativity with which they have lived. So in complex and varying ways, notions of community, race, ethnicity, gender, citizenship and migrant status played a significant role in how the Black young people in both studies thought about their educational and occupational paths and the avenues they pursued. In the case of the Jane-Finch youth, among all (Blacks, South Asians and Asians[8]) who participated in the studies I conducted, three major themes stand out in their narratives about the significance or purpose of education — and higher education in particular — in their lives. These are: (1) to contradict popular notions of themselves as low achievers, (2) to return their dues to the community and (3) to leave the community (either physically or emotionally).

Challenging the Stereotype of Themselves as Low Achievers

Up against teachers' perceptions of them as low achievers and hence "at-risk" students, the youth in the Jane-Finch community challenged these stereotypes particularly when it came to their schooling and relationships with teachers. In a recent study (James and Taylor 2010) of their schooling experiences, participants pointed out that they were routinely stereotyped as "bad" or "troublemakers" with little interest in education on the basis of their skin colour and the neighbourhood in which they lived. They reasoned that the discriminatory treatment they received from teachers was a consequence of societal stereotypes of them and their community. This treatment, they hypothesized, was further bolstered by teachers passing on information about students to other teachers. For instance, one participant, Kevin, said that his teachers thought of him as "some ultimate gangster, drug dealer person," and they would tell his "friends not to hang with me because I'm a drug dealer." To counter such action on the part of teachers, the youth would alert their peers to their experiences, claiming that they were "looking out for each other" with the knowledge that unfavourable attitudes and exclusionary practices would have a detrimental effect on their educational performance and achievements. Sandra told us how, having heard from her friends that a particular teacher "doesn't like your type of people," she would sit in front of the class and do her work with the expectation that the teacher "would pass" her. Sandra was one of the compliant students who believed that if she made the teacher see her doing her work, then that would change the teacher's opinion of her. Other students — the resistant ones — felt that it was the teachers that needed to "adjust their attitudes" and not themselves. From the perspective of these resisting students, adjusting their attitudes required teachers to acknowledge and give consideration to the reality of their students' lives beyond the classroom and the school — in doing so, teachers would get to know them.

But resisting students are well aware that if they are to have an impact on their teachers and the education system, and if they are to effectively address and change the stereotypes that exist of them as disinterested students, then they cannot have just one approach to their school problems. After all, they would have to show that young people from their community can do well academically. It is possible that it is with this idea in mind that some students, while maintaining their resistance stance, encouraged others among them to go along with the educational program in an effort to show educators and others that members of their community can graduate from high school and go on to college and university. Through their actions, the youth sought to challenge and contradict the ways educators essentialized or read them and simply lump them into a group of underachievers. In their minds, it is not that young people from their community lack the aptitude for academic work, but rather it is the failure of the education system and educators to be responsive to their needs, interests and expectations (James and Haig-Brown 2001: 238).

A case in point is Rebecca, an African Canadian, who admitted to hanging around with friends whom teachers deemed to be disengaged students. She stated that her friends were very encouraging of her decision to attend university.

> *Rebecca*: Actually, they're proud of me. A lot of them see me as their opportunity, you know what I mean, so it's like, I'm kinda the breakthrough, for some of them, you know what I mean, so I get pushed a lot from them, they understand when I can't hang out and they actually push me not to hang out and say, "Go pick up your book" or something.

> *Interviewer*: Why do you think that is?

> *Rebecca*: Because underlyingly we all want to succeed; but it's

easier to place your hopes and dreams in somebody else than be responsible for doing it yourself. (James and Haig-Brown 2001: 238)

The support that Rebecca received from her African-Canadian peers might seem to contradict their characteristic defiant behaviour toward school and teachers. But their collective support can be seen as in keeping with the way they live vicariously through each other and the fact that Rebecca's educational ambitions and "breakthrough" — that is, her achievements — convey a message to educators that young Black people from Jane and Finch are capable of attaining a university education.

Conrad and Kendra were two university students who did their best to prove that the stereotypes that were held of young people like themselves did not apply to them (James 2010b). Conrad, a Jamaican-born Black male who immigrated to Canada at age fifteen, had to contend with the regular stereotype of being more athletically than academically inclined and, as a recent immigrant, unlikely to do well in school. As a resident of Jane and Finch, he was confronted with the additional stereotype of the Black male as gang member, drug dealer and gun user. In resisting or working against this racializing, gendered profile, Conrad immersed himself into his academic work, did not consider going after an athletic scholarship despite the advice of his coach and had very little interaction with his neighbourhood peers. This is how Conrad explained his use of social distance from his peers to ensure that he remained a good student:

> *Conrad*: For me it was pretty simple. Like I went to school, went to track, went home and did my homework. Like outside school I had no friends in the area, so I don't think I had the good experience of what it was like to grow up in Jane and Finch. I was pretty isolated; even within there I was pretty much in my own world, so I didn't really, I guess, associate with a lot of people from the area outside of school.

> *Carl*: Why?

> *Conrad*: Because [of a] combination of being too busy with stuff and school, [and a] combination of not wanting to get in trouble because of its reputation, pretty much those two things.

> *Carl*: What about the reputation of [the school]?

> *Conrad*: The reputation? I don't know, I can only think of my experiences. I mean you have kids that got into trouble, probably because of the socio-economic conditions, there is probably

more than your typical school but I loved my experience at [high school]. (James 2010b: 128)

Conrad's and Kendra's approach to their schooling was obviously supported by their parents and teachers (as will be seen later) who expected them to go on to university. But as "model students" or as "good role models" trying to show that good students can come out of that community, it is possible that they unwittingly created a problem for their peers, who were perceived as "lacking the drive to do well." As long as students such as Rebecca, Conrad and Kendra succeed in such urban schools, then teachers "with good intentions," as Milner (2006) would say, will probably come to see the problems of low academic achievement, disruptive behaviours and dropping out of school as reflective of the inability of students and their parents to meet the expectations of teachers and to handle the school program. It is worth noting that while "good students" might be prepared to distance themselves from their neighbourhood peers to satisfy the expectations of their parents and teachers, other students might be unwilling to do the same because they believe the cost of doing so — that is, losing friends and disconnecting from the community and even family members — is too high (James 2010b: 134).

Returning the Dues

I have already mentioned that, for most of the young people, their university education is not merely for self-betterment or personal social mobility but is inextricably linked to "giving back" or "returning the dues" to their community (James and Haig-Brown 2001). And while the geographic area of Jane and Finch was referred to as their community, in fact it also meant, as noted by Catherine, the group of people living in the area with whom she shared the "same or common interests, ethnic background and race." Like Catherine, most of the research participants imagined their community in terms of race, ethnicity and the region from which their parents had immigrated. So the community of Jane and Finch was not conceptualized as one community but as a circumscribed geographic area made up of several ethno-racial communities. It is to these specific ethno-racial communities that students referred in their claims to knowledge of the communities they expected to serve. As Catherine states:

as I get more experience working with my community, I feel the interest to serve my community, to help them through the problems that they're having now so that's how my interest in becoming a social worker has played a part in my life because I've been so interactive with my community that I know the issue that's been affecting them and I, as a Cambodian worker, would like to serve my community as much as I could, as much as I want to be a teacher, but, you know I think it's more of me to serve my community, that's why I chose the field of social work. (James and Haig-Brown 2001: 241)

So as the students talked about entering professions in human services as a means of gaining the necessary knowledge and skills to work in and for the "community," they were well aware of the complexity and enormity of the task. Their approach to working with the community — in other words, the ethno-racial group — with which they are familiar and have solidarity is realistic. Jamaican-born Vivian, who "grew up in the area" and went to the schools there, said that she wished to teach at her former high school when she graduated because she wanted to offer students the same support she received from her high-school teachers. She indicated that initially she thought of becoming a nurse, but changed her mind because she "could offer more as a teacher, set an example as a role model, counsel, offer advice, [and] steer someone in the right direction." She believed that as a teacher she could model the idea that "I've been there and you can too." At the time of the interview, Rebecca was pursuing teaching instead of law. She suggested that

> law school is a long-term goal and I don't know if it's really practi-
> cal for me right now, because I don't want to be in school forever,
> and I don't want to be owing back the government money. But I
> think the two are intertwined for me because in my spare time
> I've always helped at the community centre and I'm always doing
> some sort of, I guess, teaching with young people, so I see it, if I
> go into the law profession I'll still be able to help my community
> because I can defend a lot of them that will be involved in the law,
> or as a high school teacher I can still prepare them and better help
> them and give them the push to go on which a lot of them don't
> get from say, other schools. (James and Haig-Brown 2001: 242)

With reference to her experience of hanging out with "the worst set of kids in [high] school...; the ones that didn't go to class," Rebecca feels that by becoming a teacher she would be able to address the schooling situation that precipitates such practices among students; for them, she will be someone who cares. Further, she anticipates that her presence will represent social and racial diversity among the teaching staff. Rebecca suggests that with someone like herself working in a school in the area, students will change their "bad attitude toward teachers," which, as she hypothesized, is a result of the fact that students are "just used to teachers that don't care, or are used to seeing teachers that aren't them, that don't live in the community." She went on to suggest that "it would be beneficial if there were more… teachers of colour, or teachers that actually lived in the neighbourhood… because Jane and Finch is a community… where things get done by people working together and like, me talking to your mother to help you out." Evidently, Rebecca's choice of law as a possible career is also related to her experiences with her high-school peers, whom she recognized as people who will potentially need legal support in their struggles with the justice system. This recognition is likely reinforced by Rebecca's awareness of the extent to which Black youths, particularly males in working-class communities such as Jane and Finch, tend to be constructed as troublemakers and criminals; hence, they are often targeted by police (James and Haig-Brown 2001: 242; see also James and Taylor 2010).

Nguyen and Sumita were two young people who talked more about working with the community as a whole and less about their respective ethno-racial communities. Nguyen, a Vietnamese refugee, also aspired to become a teacher and remain within the community. But Nguyen, grateful to be in Canada — "I came from Vietnam, and I know in a way that I was thankful to be here" — was less circumscribed to working with his ethnic community. For him, "paying back" — more precisely, "returning the dues" — was not so much about his ethnic community or Jane and Finch in particular, but about the Canadian public to whom he felt a deep sense of appreciation and commitment. Here is how Nguyen explained it:

> I am thankful to be here [in Canada], so I'm paying, well, it's not really paying back, but I want to return my dues. So if I'm not going into teaching, I'm probably going into some service field…. It's very silly, but it's deep-rooted in me that I'm thankful to be here…. So this is why business is not for me…. I think you're in business for yourself… not the community or the country. (James and Haig-Brown 2001: 239)

Nguyen's reference to business here is related to the fact that his parents had wanted him to study business, where, as he recalled, it might be "easier to get jobs… and probably make more money." But Nguyen, as he emphasized, was less concerned than his parents with making money or the prestige of business.

Sumita, of South-Asian origin, was also less concerned with working in her ethnic community. In fact, having been active in student government in high school, she planned to pursue a career in politics to "help effect change" in the community. She reasoned that a career in politics would enable her to gain "access to a resource base, people and knowledge,

[and] the ability to change things I don't like in the community." A political science major in university, she felt that she was well suited to changing the hopeless attitudes of many people in the community because "I grew up there, and I know what it needs, and what growing changes it's going through." Furthermore, Sumita understood that to bring about the needed changes would take time. As she stated, "I'm trying to stay as much as I can in the community, and York University is part of the reason" (James and Haig-Brown 2001: 234).

Teachers' perception of students' present and future roles within their community were also important to the constructed aspirations of some students. The "high-achieving students" whom teachers observed to be actively participating in community activities were expected and encouraged by their teachers to pursue university education and return to "give back" to the community. For example, Rebecca reported that her teachers "pushed" her to go to university. When asked why, she said:

> Because I've always been involved with the community, and I've always, since I was twelve years old, I've always been doing something at the community centre, and like when they spoke to me on that individual level they found out that stuff, and they helped me to further my dreams, to better help my community, and so forth, and I think, too, they truly believed that I would be someone to come back and help the community, not just go off and just forget where I came from, which is something I've always stressed. (James and Haig-Brown 2001: 237)

Getting Out of the Community (Socially, Emotionally and Physically)

For the most part, the youth — some more than others — were highly invested in the goal of helping to address the needs of the community, including the stigmatized views that outsiders hold of the community. While the dominant narrative among them tended to be that of "giving back" to their community, for some students it meant working and continuing to live in the community. For most of them, it simply meant working in occupations through which they might contribute to the community, but not necessarily living there. This idea of segregated obligation — an obligation not necessarily to their teachers, but to their community and to themselves in terms of their own betterment and social mobility — has been something into which they have been socialized by their parents and other members of their community. That socialization, as they seem to recognize, has provided them with the capital — social, cultural, aspirational, navigational, familial and resistant (see Yosso 2005) — upon which they have drawn to gain the knowledge, abilities and skills to negotiate and resist the social and educational systems. They have sustained a high level of aspiration and achievement "despite the presence of stressful events and conditions that place them at risk" of possible failure (80).

Rebecca, for example, was one student who understood that the community was a place to leave. She recalled being sent to a high school outside of the school district by her Guyanese mother rather than to her local one. Similarly, while Nancy's Jamaican-born mother did not raise questions regarding Nancy's decision to attend the local high school, her elementary school teachers did suggest that she attend a school outside of the community. These examples illustrate that for some parents and educators, schooling, and by extension, social relationships with peers in the community, were problematic. Hence, they sought to remove these youth from their working-class, stigmatized community with the knowledge that schools and peers elsewhere would provide a more productive and successful educational environment. In essence, the message to the students with "potential" was that the community was one that they were to eventually leave if they were to actualize their personal ambitions.

With such socialization, there is little wonder that some young people would have somewhat ambivalent feelings toward, and fairly tenuous connections to, the community. As such, they would work at preparing themselves to eventually leave. But how do you sever ties to the community structures that are responsible for what you have and will become, and from which you draw needed support? The ideas and experiences of Conrad and Kendra are instructive here. Recall that these two mid-twenties African Canadians were university students who had attended the local high school and distanced themselves socially and emotionally from their peers and the community. As noted earlier, Conrad lived a "pretty isolated" life while in high school, as he said, not associating "with a lot of people from the area outside of school." Yet while in high school, Conrad did run for president of the student council but lost; and as a university student, he made it a point to regularly visit his former high school (on the invitation of his teachers) to speak with Grade 9 students about the need to apply themselves to their school work in order to be successful. Kendra's activities outside of school were mostly with friends from her old neighbourhood, her church and island association, where she played a leadership role helping to organize youth activities. In high school, she helped to plan Black History Month and Kwanzaa events and, in her final year, tutored Grade 9 students. While both Kendra and Conrad recognized that as residents of the community they were implicated in its reputation, they nevertheless sought to distance themselves from the other residents and avoid any trouble. On the one hand, it seems logical that students such as Conrad, Kendra and others, with the encouragement of their parents and teachers, would draw back from their community in anticipation of leaving it. On the other hand, leaving the community seems inconsistent with and contradictory to their expressed interest in giving back to it. As they indicate, it takes the experience of living in the community to know its concerns and needs, and thus prepare them to be responsive to them. Conrad, for example, said, "I think it's important that people see people from Jane and Finch who don't fit the stereotypical mode.... So if you can break that, or if I can help break that perception just by myself, then I have done something" (James 2010b: 128–129). The young people who plan to leave the community shared the views of outsiders that Jane and Finch is a mean and troubled community — a community from which to escape. But they were not "outsiders," ignorant of the community's issues. In fact, they adeptly used their lived experiences in the community to analyze the situation and to assess what needed to be done to remove the stigma. It is also possible that these students' interest in changing the popular "bad" perception of the community has to do with their desire for the reputation of the community to not be a burden to them or a barrier to their aspirations (see also College Student Alliance et al. 2011).

The logical yet inconsistent and contradictory positions that students held about leaving the community are in part influenced by their parents' support for such a move — a move that is sometimes woven into the family narrative. Some of the support from parents as well as community members (and teachers, as will be discussed in the next section) is conveyed through references to individuals who have "made it out" of the community — people who are to be admired and emulated. With such support, these parents communicate values about the limitations of the neighbourhood, its people and institutions, and, in doing so, likely legitimized the views of outsiders (and, of course, some insiders).[9] In addition, parents conveyed the message that their children's achievement in life is primarily a product of their individual effort rather than that of institutions (such as schools, social service agencies, correctional facilities, etc.) and the socio-political structures that these institutions help to preserve.

The Role of Teachers and the University in Their Schooling

As mentioned above, some teachers, like some parents, seemed to believe that one of the ways of supporting their academically successful students in their ambitions is by helping them to think of life — their own life — beyond the boundaries of Jane and Finch. To this end, teachers employed a variety of strategies such as recruiting "role models" for their students, mentoring students, acting as "stand-in parents," encouraging students to attend university and college, and simply being good, concerned teachers.

Paul, a teacher-candidate who was placed at a school in the Jane-Finch community, recalled his first meeting with his mentor teacher:

> In front of the whole group, she said to us: "It is important for you two Black gentlemen to be here. You should go out of your way... to help a lot of the Black kids along, and make it known to them that you are available.... You guys are going to be role models whether you like it or not... and it's very important that you realize what being a role model is. (James 1997: 167)

Community members, parents and educators argue that if Black students' difficulties and educational needs are to be effectively addressed, then it is necessary for them to have, or be exposed to, role models and mentors. Indeed, Paul did go on to say that he welcomed the opportunity to be a role model for the Black students; it is one of the reasons why he was in teaching. Paul, like some of the students to whom he was to become a "role model," saw this as an opportunity to give back to "his community"; it was just that his reference was to the larger Black community of metropolitan Toronto and not that circumscribed by geographic boundaries (see James 2005). But the dilemma with role models — especially in the case of Black males — as I argue elsewhere, is the uncritical and problematic ways in which the idea is taken up and practised without sufficient consideration being given to the differences (sometimes insurmountable) between the mentors (or role models) and their mentees (James and Haig-Brown 2001).

I am not saying that the students do not need, or will not benefit from, role models and mentors. Clearly, there are important roles that teachers and others have played in supporting young people as they work to achieve their aspirations. But not everyone presented as a role model or mentor will be considered as such by the youth. And contrary to Paul's mentor teacher (and others), race or perceived "cultural similarity" does not necessarily determine whom the students wish to have, or who will be identified, as their mentors. Take the case of Conrad, for example. Conrad explained that many of the teachers who helped him were Caribbean or of Caribbean descent. And because of their Caribbean background, one might assume that these teachers would have been able to appreciate and understand Conrad's situation as an immigrant student. One such teacher was Mr. Basil. But Conrad's favourite teacher, whom Conrad described as one of the few teachers who took the time to see that he did well, was not Mr. Basil, but Mr. Norman, "who is actually not a Black teacher, [but] a White teacher." Mr. Norman became Conrad's mentor, and he valued him as such partly "because he was the pickiest teacher I ever had." It was Mr. Norman whom Conrad credited with giving him the educational skills — "skills to see his mistakes and... the ability to correct them" — that helped him through high school. Conrad suggests that being a good teacher has little to do with ancestry or cultural background. His chosen mentor teachers "were just good teachers who actually cared about students" and were willing to "go out of their way to teach, and see... students for what they are, and try... to deal with those students for what they are" (James 2010b: 130).

Kendra too found her White teachers more useful to her than her Black teachers. She found them more "generous and supportive." For that reason, she would go to them first if she had a problem, even though she had "a good rapport with Black teachers" and "got along" with many of them. Of her Black teachers, she said:

> I remember just being in school, and I think it's partly why I wanted to become a teacher as well. I found that some Black teachers seemed mean, and I don't know if it was because they wanted to push the Black students harder to make sure that they achieve.... Actually, I found that the White ones pushed me more to do, like I guess, more controversial topics than my Black teachers; at least they seemed more interested. It wasn't just because I'm a Black student and you are a Black teacher that I would have this overarching bond. (James 2010b: 128)

In her comment, Kendra tries to disrupt the binary thinking inherent in the presumption of the "overarching bond" between Black students and Black teachers that is so much a part of the predominant multicultural discourse in schools and society generally. Moreover, Kendra's comments, like Conrad's comments earlier, illustrate that they are not colour-blind; race does matter, particularly in ways related to the existing schooling context and social situation. So while Kendra was put off by some Black teachers' "meanness" and was encouraged by White teachers who pushed her to work on "more controversial topics," and Conrad saw the benefits of the "pickiness" of a White teacher, the fact remains that they understand race and, by extension, racism to be factors in their interactions.

While these "upwardly mobile" students' responses might be related to their particular teaching and learning preferences, what they also signal here is complexity — race "sameness" is not the only characteristic that is significant to teacher-student relationships in their community, for race does not bridge the class differences that exist between teachers and students. According to Conrad, middle-class Black teachers

> like to think that they face the same ills as lower class Blacks because they are Black. But that is not the case. Black students are not going to listen to Black teachers from suburbia... just because they are Black; because they... don't turn on the TV every day

and hear something negative about Jane and Finch. They don't face living in the community where there are people around them who they know sell drugs, who they know have weapons, who they know are dangerous, and living in that community with the expectation, that's the lifestyle, that's an acceptable life. They don't face being third-generation welfare people.... And they don't face the low expectation that a lot of kids from Jane and Finch face, and I don't know if they can relate to that. They probably can if they get away from the whole idea of "just because I'm Black, I'm going to help." Or "just because I'm Black, I'm better suited to help." I don't know if that's completely true. (James 2010b: 131–132)

It is not sufficient to be a Black teacher; a teacher must acknowledge the differences between their middle-class "suburban" existence and the "dangers" their students face in their community (see Dippo and James 2011; Hidalgo 1997; Odih 2002). Young people such as Conrad and Kendra expected their teachers to understand, or at least try to understand, the issues and conditions in which they lived — with drugs, weapons, welfare, low expectations and media images — and appreciate that these things affected their schooling, educational lives and outcomes.

Furthermore, Conrad insisted that there was no "typical Jane-Finch" or "typical Black" student: "Some may decide to go to university when they are done, or some decide to go to college or some decide to get jobs" (James 2010b: 131). For this reason, he continued, teachers needed to think of students from the area as "pretty smart, but just because of socio-economic conditions, lack of drive, their status, the way they see themselves in the country, they just don't do well." In working with many of these "pretty smart" students, or as Sumita put it, "high-achieving students who'll be social movers and shakers"[10] and encouraging them in their educational and occupational ambitions, teachers promoted the idea of them returning to the community after university to "give back," to change things and to become role models. It is possible, then, that the students' aspirations to enter professions such as teaching, social work and law, and their linking of these aspirations to "giving back" to their community, are more constructions of their teachers' aspirations for them than their own — but aspirations to which they eventually acquiesced out of a sense of respect for and loyalty to their teachers, obligation to their parents and community expectations.

The Westview Partnership was a convenient resource for teachers in their bid to place post-secondary education within the students' reach. In fact, the various partnership programs exposed students to role models, mentors, career clubs (e.g., Future Teachers' Club), university campus life through visits to the university and an Advance Credit Experience, which selected Grade 11 and 12 students were able to take. Besides, given York University's proximity to the Jane-Finch community — a short bus ride or a fifteen-minute walk gets one onto the campus — it is understandable that, with such exposure, over a period of time, the students from the area would begin to think of the university as part of their community. And, as Rebecca was inspired to say when reflecting on the Advance Credit course she had taken at the university, "I was like, if this is what university is about, then I can handle this because some of the stuff we [covered] in the course was really something I could relate to.... This was good, if this is what university is about. It wasn't like I perceived it to be, which was a lot of meaningless hard work" (James and Haig-Brown 2001: 236). The students also came to identify the university as "a community resource," with the post-secondary programs they wanted. But the idea of "getting out" of the community also played a role in the universities and colleges that students attended. I have met students who have not attended York University because they wanted to get away from Jane and Finch.

Before leaving this discussion of the teachers' role in influencing students about the role they should play in the future of the community, it is worth noting that there is something troubling about it. There are indeed many good and practical reasons for the young people of the community to become role models and to give back to it. However, having internalized the discourse of giving back and making it so much a part of their own narrative, it is possible that the young people may become blind to its possible negative consequences. And despite their good intentions, teachers, likely oblivious to the limitations of their expectation, could be seen as individuating the problems of the community, leading the students to think that it is their problem and theirs to solve.

Conclusion

The research conducted over the years with young people from the Jane and Finch community showed that they faithfully banked on education as the means by which to fully participate in the society, to realize their economic and social goals and to change outsiders' negative perceptions of their community. The students drew on their experiences and understanding of their community in relation to their class, ethno-racial and immigrant backgrounds to construct and sustain their high educational and career aspirations. For the most part, supported by their parents and teachers, the young people recognized that their attendance at university was necessary for them to realize their career aspirations, to get out of the neighbourhood, to give back to their community and to work toward changing outsiders' view of their neighbourhood. Even those young people considered to be educationally disengaged or "at-risk" students admitted to the importance and benefits of education, not only for themselves but also for the reputation of the community and/or specific ethno-racial group (see also Bourke and Jayman 2010; Cammarota and Fine 2008).

Most of the young people were confident that they had what it takes to realize their ambitions. "You have to believe in yourself to achieve [your ambitions]," said Kendra. "If something is not going right for you, find ways to change it. I do know that racism is out there, and I've experienced subtle things but not anything that will stop me — at least right now — from going through [with] what I want to do" (James 2010b: 127). This resoluteness, determination, and social and cultural capital, together with their belief in the meritocratic, democratic and emancipatory promise of education, appear to contribute to their notion that the education and occupations to which they aspire will leverage their marginalization and dispel the stigma of their community. They seemed to share a mindset that structural barriers such as classism and racism that operated to restrict or limit their opportunities are things that they would be able to overcome through hard work and perseverance. Their mantra of "Anything is possible" was a recurring theme in their narrative. "You can allow things to govern your life or you can deal with them then and just kind of move on," said Conrad.

Paradoxically, while questioning and challenging the insularity of educational institutions and some of their teachers, a number of the young people also complied with the very principles and practices that maintained the insularity. And in their compliance, acting as or planning to act as role models and mentors and by attending university, they demonstrated that the Eurocentric, middle-class, individualist ethos of education was not a barrier to their achievements. With community solidarity and affinity as helpful coping mechanisms, the young people cultivated the values, beliefs and behaviours that helped to make possible high educational and occupational goals while also breaking through barriers, resulting in upward social mobility. Their educational hopes are reflective of their sense of obligation to both their family and their community. In that context, education was read as valuable for its ability to simultaneously meet the needs of their family and community while also contributing to their own betterment. In essence, education, particularly post-secondary, was regarded (or framed) as possessing the necessary tools to level the playing field as opposed to being seen as the great inequitable gatekeeper.

Notes

1. The original Westview Partnership was with the North York Board of Education. When the respective school boards in Metropolitan Toronto were amalgamated, the Partnership continued with the existing Toronto District School Board. The Advance Credit Experience (ACE) program has been operating as part of the Partnership involving the Toronto District School Board, the Toronto Catholic District School Board schools, Seneca College and York University. For a period, this program was financially supported by the Ontario Ministry of Training, Colleges and Universities, the York Faculty Association and private donors. The program has significantly increased the number of students from the Jane-Finch area now attending university or college.

2. One of the University Path Program's offerings was the Future Teachers' Club, in which students who aspired to become teachers participated. There they were mentored by teachers and teacher-candidates.

3. All the names used in the discussion of the studies are pseudonyms.

4. About eight youth participated in each focus group.

5. It is worth noting that many of the youth in the Jane and Finch area have immigrant parents and grandparents. This means that, even as first-, second- and third-generation Canadians, they are not far removed from the hardworking, high-aspirations ethos — the "immigrant drive" — of their parents and their parents' belief that it is through education that they and/or their children will be able to attain the social mobility that they seek through the act of immigrating to Canada (Anisef et al. 2000).

6. They are all of African-Caribbean background.

7. Their birthplaces or those of their parents were Ghana, St. Vincent, Jamaica and Guyana.

8. As mentioned above, these participants are of Vietnamese, Cambodian, Sri Lankan and Indian backgrounds.

9. For instance, Kendra reported that her "strict" father insisted that she not associate with neighbourhood peers — an attitude that helped depict the community as dangerous.

10. Sumita also pointed out that she felt "pressured to go to university" by her teachers, "guessing" that "when you're a high achieving student, and you're very involved extra-curricularly and in the community and stuff like that, the expectation is immediately university, and college tends to get a bad rap" (James and Haig-Brown 2001: 237).

Chapter 5

Anatomy of a School Shooting

On May 23, 2007, Canadian newscasts reported that a student had been shot in a Toronto high-school hallway. The public's reaction was one of horror and outrage. This was yet another major incident in which Torontonians were left to wonder about the presence of guns in the city. The other notable shooting — one that had capped the "year of the gun" of 2005 — was the Boxing Day incident on Yonge Street in downtown Toronto. These two shooting incidents not only tapped into the fears individuals had for their own safety, but also unravelled the delicate threads of Toronto's Canadian multicultural identity. While in 2005 Toronto had confronted the horrors of gun violence and grew cynical, the high-school shooting in 2007 brought new and fresh terrors. This time a "sacred" space in a "good" school was violated, a space where the youth of Canada spend the greater part of their days.[1]

Jordan Manners, fifteen years of age, died from a gunshot wound to the chest. Four days later the public learned that Jordan's schoolmates, his "friends," were suspects. The arrest of two male students, only two years his senior, made the shocking incident more baffling and therefore much more captivating. Everyone wondered, "What would lead them to shoot a fellow student in the very school that they all attended?" and there were concerns for the lack of regard young people seem to have for life.[2] Accordingly, everyone searched for answers. The implications of Jordan's death — what it revealed and what it says about us — are difficult to justify and explain, partly because the implications are still unfolding. Ostensibly, when Jordan Manners died we not only mourned for him, but also for ourselves, for all that we would have to confront, and for the future of the city, our communities and our schools.

Jordan's death instigated vigorous debates around major social and political issues pertaining to schooling, education and life in disadvantaged urban neighbourhoods. It precipitated inquests, investigations, reports, theses, journal articles and even book chapters. It alerted us, as O'Grady, Parnaby and Schikschneit (2010: 70) argue, to how the media ignore "the complex and changing life experiences of people who find themselves living in difficult circumstances."[3] The death has affected how we see, experience and think of schooling and educational programs now and for the future, and how we recall past ones. The tragedy also exposed how public institutions failed to cooperate with one another and made plain how some students manage to "slip through the cracks." Mostly, it shed light on how we, as a society and as individuals, are implicated in the schooling situation and community life of our youth. In this regard, we offer a reading of the paradoxes, contradictions, myths and the myriad of issues the shooting opened up. What does it mean for a "gifted child" and a "good school" to exist in a "stigmatized" community? How do religious values and police presence in schools operate to maintain obedience and safety? What does the fatherless discourse do to help explain what is wrong with today's Black youth? And how can measures such as mentorship programs and a focused school help to culturally respond to the needs of the youth and hence avoid further incidents?

A "Good" Child from a "Troubled" Community

The image of a young person with dreams and determination cut down "well before" his or her time makes for a good news story. Despite the coldness of this reality, such a portrayal serves multiple purposes. Perhaps the first is that of courtesy or convention. It is thought to be disrespectful to "speak ill of the dead." So any aspects of the deceased's life that could be considered "negative" are at times glossed over or altogether omitted.[4] The second is that the image helps to give permission to constrained sorrow and anger. The life of a child is inherently worthy, full of promise, and so the loss is more pronounced. Unsavoury details ought not to get in the way of the public's right to an uncomplicated sympathetic emotional reaction. The third is that the portrayal of death is shaped by cultural and social norms and ideals and practices. Victims are typically described as hardworking, ambitious or nice, and we are reminded, sometimes not so gently, that these characteristics are what we all should possess. These claims conspire to idolize the victim to elicit a more enduring public sympathy. Therefore, our effort to find out who Jordan was, to honour his brief and unfinished life, came not only from the impulse to grieve and find value in grieving, but also to ensure that that our grief was merited. And the fact that he knew his perpetrators — that his death was not random — meant that we and our children were not in any personal danger since the incident was contained to, and within, "the distant" community.

Interestingly, while Torontonians mourned Jordan's death, their nagging questions and doubts lingered. And despite the many things that worked in his favour, the questions persisted. He was not shot late at night on a dangerous street or outside of a packed nightclub, but in the hallways of a high school. Even so, questions (such as "Why was he not in class?") lingered in the minds of many and were voiced in hushed tones or explicitly (see note 2) — questions that cast aspersions on many young Black males in relation to incidents of truancy and violence. But there were other questions informed by Jordon's age, gender, race and family composition, as well as his neighbourhood. He was young, male and Black. And, despite the statistical reality that young Black men are disproportionately victimized by violent crime, we are much more likely to know about, and hence conceive of, these youth as perpetrators. Aside from his race and age, another more ominous suspicion loomed. Jordan lived in Jane and Finch. And given the prevailing perceptions of the community — in part, facilitated by the media — it was not enough for Jordan be a typical young male person; he had to be different, that is, a young person with the potential to "go somewhere" (i.e., out of Jane and Finch). Jordan had to be as good as the community was bad. This became the framework for Jordan's story.

It started with photographs. The photograph of Jordan most frequently used was of his Grade 8 graduation. From the cover of Toronto's major daily newspapers, and on the screens of local television news broadcasts, stared a fresh-faced boyish-looking Black youth. He wore braids and was light skinned, possibly of European and African parentage. The picture enshrined him in our consciousness as a student — a successful one. The initial descriptions of Jordan that made it into the news supported such a reading. Fellow students characterized him as a "gifted drama student," "popular" and "well-liked." In the *Toronto Star*, Rosie DiManno (2007a) described Jordan as a fifteen-year-old boy from Jane and Finch who wrote poems and drew nature pictures and showed, from all indications, that he was a jewel, someone who could rise successfully from these mean and impoverished surroundings. In a CityTV interview on May 23, his aunt said, "He was not a bad person. Not everyone that lives in Jane and Finch is in a gang or has a gun. There are a lot of good people who live here and Jordan was one of those people." Also, his mother repeatedly reminded us that Jordan had had no prior contact with the law. Everyone involved knew that there was plenty at stake and accordingly made it clear that Jordan was different. He was special and an exception to the "norm."[5]

The "special child," the one who tries to transcend his origins, is an old and very common archetype. Here, it is used to invoke social concern about a youth. It not only separates him from, but simultaneously degrades, the social environment that produced him. As DiManno (2007b) writes, "The gifted child had his art, his theatricals, his poems, his love for nature, his passion for basketball; he planted trees in the ravine behind his school and built birdcages that still hang in those boughs. He oozed self-confidence, a youth going places, didn't matter where he'd started out." By portraying Manners as a "jewel" trapped in a "mean and impoverished" community, the media and even other community residents "inadvertently" characterized other youth as not as capable and not so worthy of our support.

Some media reports went so far as to pronounce those other young people as "spiritually dead." In "redeeming" this victim, the media used and deepened the stigmatization of Jane and Finch. In the *Globe and Mail*, the neighbourhood was described as a place where people "long endured violent outbreaks of street crime" related to gangs that operated in the community (O'Grady, Parnaby and Schikschneit 2010: 62). The better and more incredible Jordan seemed, the more horrible Jane and Finch became.[6] Given the outcry and the "atypical" nature of Jordan's death, answers had to be found and opportunities created to address the underlying needs, issues and assumptions that precipitate such tragedies.

However, while caught up in the captivating drama of the shooting, the public somehow failed to recognize the resilience and resourcefulness of the community despite its "impoverishment." Also overlooked was our complicity in the social and economic problems (structured by racism, classism, xenophobia, etc.) and the failure of our society to effectively attend to the educational, social and economic needs of its youth and their families. Moreover, a community plagued by poverty and populated by hardworking, ambitious individuals is a community oppressed by structural inequity and injustice. What happens in that community and with the residents is not merely a consequence of their own making but is something in which we are all complicit.

A "Good" School in a "Poor" Area

In early media reports, Jordan's school was described as a "good" school, but later, in connecting it to the Jane-Finch community, that classification changed. CTV noted that "the school has about 850 students and is located near the Jane and Finch corridor, a poor area of Toronto noted for years for its high crime rate" (CTV 2007). Such reports indicate that students from the community attend the school and were affected by its problems. But it was considered a safe school — a school to which parents sent their children with the hope that they would be able to avoid the "risks" associated with the community. In fact, even after the shooting, the students continued to consider the school to be safe. Findings from the inquiry conducted after the shooting indicate that three out of every four students (or 75 percent) felt that "their school is either very safe (29 percent) or fairly safe (45 percent)" (Falconer, Edwards and MacKinnon 2008: 34). While these students' responses might be a reflection of their recognition that their future is tied to the school's reputation, it is also likely a reflection of their understanding that it is the institution on which they are dependent if they are to "escape" (or get out of) the neighbourhood and realize their educational and occupational ambitions.

The life and death of Chevon "Sheisty" Josephs can perhaps portray the necessity for schools to be responsive to the differential needs and expectations of minority male youth in "poor" neighbourhoods before they go down a path of destruction, or enter the prison pipeline (see Farmer 2010; Krueger 2010; Meiners and Winn 2010); a trip that affects not only their own lives, but also the lives of others. On the heels of Manners' death, in early June of 2007, fifteen-year-old Josephs crashed a stolen car into a taxi while fleeing the police. He died in the crash. So did the taxi's two Black female (sixteen- and seventeen-year-old) passengers. All three young people were from the Jane-Finch area. At Josephs' funeral, his aunts recalled his troubles in school: "When Chevon started school, it was clear to see it would be a challenge" (Srikanthan 2007). They went on to say that his teachers described him as "a capable, smart student when he applied himself" in elementary school. But things changed. High school proved to be difficult for Josephs as "he wasn't always able to stand strong against the negative pressures and temptations that young kids now face." But that didn't deter him from going to school, they said, because he knew his job was to finish his education. Josephs aunts' comments highlight the issue at hand in the case of many young Black men involved in the death and tragedies that occurred in Jane and Finch in 2007. Many of these youth — whether victims or perpetrators — were sadly disengaged from school and, as a consequence, remained deeply enmeshed in the struggle against poverty, racism, stigmatization and their "at-risk" designation.

There is no doubt that many attempts have been made to locate and frame the source of the problem facing minority males, particularly those (Africans/Blacks, Latin Americans, Aboriginals and Portuguese) who are estimated to drop out of Toronto schools at a rate of about 40 percent (McKell 2010). Many of these students are classified as "at-risk" students[7] — assessed through a combination of standardized test scores, behavioural matters and tests for specific learning problems and/or disabilities. But these tests and the application of the "at-risk" label are influenced by the ethos and structure of inequity in relation to class, gender, race, language, immigrant status and family composition (James 2012). And, often lost in the assessment process are the classist, masculinist, heterosexist and racist assumptions that inform the interpretations made of students and of their parents' capacity to provide the necessary supports, guidance and discipline. It is questionable, then, whether the "at-risk" marker actually gets students the help they really need as opposed to stigmatizing them, particularly in relation to their community. Hence, when something like a shooting takes place in a school, much will be said about "at-risk" students (indeed, much was said about Manners and his peers) — not only about their academic and social needs, but also about their lack of discipline.

In such a context, having police in school patrolling the halls was seen as a welcomed initiative, especially among teachers.

The Policing of Schools

Concerned about the safety of students as well as teachers, educators attempted to address the perceived violence in schools. A number of surveillance measures were contemplated and some put in place in a number of schools in Toronto and elsewhere. But whereas it seemed reasonable for police to visit schools as they patrol the neighbourhoods, Jane-Finch community members — while unanimously concerned about their children's safety — were spilt on the question of having police officers in their schools. This question was vigorously debated, as evidenced in discussions by people who attended community meetings and others who expressed their opinions in informal polls on videos posted to YouTube (Jane-Finch.com 2009). Some argued that the presence of police would provide a level of safety and security to students and teachers, making the schooling environment more conducive to learning. Others argued that the presence of police in schools could instead cause students to be anxious, thereby making the environment even less hospitable for learning and possibly resulting in students choosing not to attend. Opponents also argued that a potential consequence of police presence in schools is the criminalization of students, which would contribute to the reputed school-to-prison pipeline. Generally, there was a fear that the presence of police would give the impression that the school is "bad," thereby validating the stigma of the community. What community members wished for were more social service staff to look after the social and emotional welfare of students.

The opposition to police presence in Jane-Finch neighbourhood schools is influenced by, among other things, residents' longstanding "distrust" of police, as well as their perception of the community as being "over-policed." Moreover, residents seemed justified in opposing the presence of police in the schools, since the Safety Panel that was appointed by the Toronto District School Board (TDSB) to investigate school safety after the shooting did not recommend this practice (Falconer, Edwards and MacKinnon 2008). For their part, the youth were concerned about being under the close observing eyes of police who, as one youth put it, "would force their authority on us" (Jane-Finch.com 2009). It was also observed that a small incident in school could escalate, resulting in a youth being charged and receiving "a criminal record" — a situation that could lead to students dropping out of school at higher rates than previously.

But as a Toronto Staff Sergeant contended, following a November 24, 2008, community meeting (Jane-Finch.com 2008) held at one of the neighbourhood high schools, School Resource Officers (SROs), as they are called, are not in the schools "to patrol the halls, run metal detectors, seize weapons, or arrest kids." Instead, he insisted that the officers — many of them currently in Toronto schools — are "there to build relationships" with students. In this regard, they participate in activities such as school trips, camping, basketball games, school dances and parent-teacher nights. The officer went on to say: "We are not here to put armed officers in the school, to criminalize kids, or arrest kids…. [People] should look beyond the outside, look beyond the uniform, look beyond the gun and see the person. We wear a uniform. We wear a gun; it's the tool of the trade. It's not the only thing that defines us."[8]

Despite objections from the community, today, School Resource Officers are patrolling the hallways of schools in the Jane-Finch neighbourhood, as they are in other urban and suburban schools (particularly high schools) in the Greater Toronto Area. In addition to police officers, the hallways of schools are also patrolled by "hall monitors" or "safety monitors." Seemingly conscious of what School Safety Monitors represent, school administrators try to capitalize on their skills and other resources. For instance, in a recent *Toronto Star* article, reporter Louise Brown (2011a) related that the four School Safety Monitors working in one of the high schools in Jane and Finch were "more mentor than muscle." Brown writes:

> On top of keeping the school safe, these hall monitors now coach basketball, accompany boys on an annual leadership retreat in Muskoka and run an auto club that has awakened interest in apprenticeships. They help drive students to local grade schools to read to younger children, and oversee a gym free-for-all lunch…. They even have designed a way to help suspended teens get back on track.

One School Safety Monitor is quoted in the article as saying, "We're like walking counsellors; we can tell when kids are starting to go off track as they start to skip class or smoke or not wear their school uniform or disrespect women…. And we can sit down and talk to them, sometimes all day."

If the truth be told, concerns about school safety are premised, in part, on the assumption that today's students are failing to live lives informed by Judeo-Christian principles and values — something that is occasionally expressed by community members.

The Call to Return to Judeo-Christian Values and Practices

At Jordan Manners' well-attended funeral service, the preacher exhorted those in attendance to look inside themselves and to come back to the church to fix what was wrong with them and their communities. Of course, touched by the tragedy, and looking for explanations, members of the congregation were likely ready for what might be seen as a solution to what ails them. Hence, it is understandable that, as *Toronto Star* reporter Rosie DiManno (2007a) noted, the congregation would give "the loudest ovation" to Jordan's grandfather when he "called for the Lord's Prayer to be taught again in schools." Indeed, when overwhelmed by change, people would likely desire to return to, or reinvent, tradition. And for many people, particularly members of the Black community for whom traditional Judeo-Christian values provide solace in their time of grief, a return to religious values is likely to have been seen as key to ending violence in the communities.

Critics might say that such solace offers dubious, vague guidance, but alternative responses are scarce and so it is accepted with fleeting support and enthusiasm. In fact, before May 2007, in 2005, local religious leaders held marches and press conferences to try and bring about change in the tradition of Martin Luther King Jr. They invited Reverent Eugene Rivers, a Black Bostonian pastor, to help diagnose Toronto's ills. In a *Globe and Mail* article, he asserted that absent fathers, "thug life" and a "failure of leadership from the Black middle and upper classes... contributes to gang-related violence in the ghettos" (2005: A23). Rivers prescribed more church involvement in social programming and greater presence in "at-risk" communities. There had been some attempts to address the problems through the initiation of a number of youth-oriented social organizations and programs, most of which were precariously funded.

Manners' death seemed to have prepared people for more of the same religious advice and perhaps more social service programs supported by religious and faith communities. It heralded a resurgence of neighbour-hood marches led by Black religious leaders in marginalized communities that had not been seen since 2005 — the so-called "year of the gun." The shooting also spawned a renewed examination of the relationship between family composition and the problems of young people. Particular reference was made to single mothers, who are typically thought to lack the abil-ity to effectively care for and discipline their children — especially their teenage boys. The subtext is that fathers are neglectful, irresponsible and for the most part absent.

Single Mothers, Fatherlessness and "Broken Homes"
In the wake of Jordan's death, the *Toronto Star* published "Where Are the Men?", a report by its National Affairs' reporter Linda Diebel (2007: A1). The report examined the "hidden crisis" within Black families in poor communities resulting from the absence of fathers. Diebel attended a

mentorship meeting where she observed that there were few men gathered; but there was Jeff Renford, whom she described as "a burly man with a Jamaican lilt" and "a mission to save kids from drugs and gangs in our city." She also interviewed single mothers who lived in public housing complexes. Referring to Statistics Canada 2001 Census data, Diebel noted that 44 percent of Black children lived in low-income families, compared to only 19 percent of other children; and almost 50 percent of Black children ages fourteen years and under lived in single-parent families, compared to only one-fifth of other children.[9] Diebel also cited a study that followed 6,000 males between the ages of fourteen and twenty-two between 1978 and 1993. It revealed that an absent father doubles a young man's chance of ending up in prison. Missing from the presentation of this data was a critical exploration of the underlying factors — specifically, the systemic factors — that account for the so-called "hidden crisis" among Black young men in low-income communities.

Indeed, read uncritically, the heart-wrenching horror stories point to a dire situation in which the youth and their single mothers find themselves largely as a result of individual moral failures. But the systemic inequities that mediate the economic opportunities and outcomes of individuals cannot be disregarded. For instance, we know that single mothers have to combine home and employment responsibilities — sometimes working at more than one job in order to make ends meet — in a context where affordable housing, access to education, job flexibility and equitable pay remain elusive for many. The seemingly logical and validating (and sensationally appealing) stories that Diebel tells were hardly novel or unique. In fact, a few months earlier, a similar approach had been taken by CBC Radio.

It was in early 2007, ironically or deliberately during Black History Month, that CBC Radio aired the series "Growing Up Without Men," hosted by Andy Barrie. Participating in the program were mostly male educators, researchers and community activists, as well as young men who testified about their experiences of "growing up without fathers." A number of the guests cited studies that linked the breakdown of the nuclear family with criminality and delinquent behavior (CBC Radio 2007). David Popenoe, for instance, stated that "the most widely reported statistic is that a child growing up without two parents has about twice the risk in life of having serious problems." And Dr. Eugene Rivers, the African-American religious leader, offered the following: "John J. Dilulio of the University of Pennsylvania has presided over a series of empirical studies that document that father absence is the single most important predictor of whether or not a kid is going to get involved in forms of anti-social activity." In his contribution to the CBC program, Dr. Chris Spence, currently the director of the Toronto District School Board and founder/creator of Boys2Men — a mentorship program designed to help disengaged boys — said that it is possible over the course of a year of working with boys to identify those who "didn't have dads." According to Dr. Spence, they tend to be

> angry young men with little or no respect for themselves or others, poor academic skills, poor life skills, limited problem solving skills. And what we saw was they really viewed school as temporary incarceration. They were there to hang out, have fun with no focus, no engagement in school whatsoever.

There is a perception in the larger society that, among Black people, single-motherhood is not imbued with the same moral stigma because it is somewhat of a norm within "Black culture." The implication is that Black cultural attitudes and values are responsible. Andy Barrie, host of *Metro Morning*, prompted Dr. Rivers in his interview with the following:

> Let's talk about the romanticizing if we could. I'm looking at the lyrics to a song called Baby Mamma: "Nowadays, it's a badge of honour to be a baby mamma. I see you paying your bills, I see you working your job, I see you going to school… and girl, I know it's hard, and even though I know you're fed up with making beds, you're a hero."
>
> Talk to me about the culture of music, and the culture…. Again, we had a young woman on this morning, and she was saying that everywhere she goes with three children fathered by two different men, people tell her she's doing an exemplary job…. They try to turn her into a hero.

In his interview with Dr. Jeffrey Johnson, citing writers such as Alice Walker and Toni Morrison, Barrie also made the argument that "young black women in a sense feel overconfident" to the extent that they have taken a position that they do "not need black men."

Seemingly, a major focus of the series "Growing Up Without Men" was the moral responsibility of parents and members of "Black communities." What the series failed to engage was the role of the historical, economic, social and cultural structures in the lives of women who become single mothers. Professor Orlando Patterson, an American scholar, was one of the interviewees on the program. He did mention the weight of systemic factors on family structures of descendents of the trans-Atlantic slave trade and how their experiences have shaped today's realities. Patterson referred to the 1960s as a time when women were able to move out of their homes for "better job opportunities in the urban setting" and as a consequence gained a level of independence. He continued, "And it's very significant that one of the main reasons that you have such low marriage rates is not just men being irresponsible parents, but it's women saying the men are high risk and they don't want to get married." Like their African-American counterparts, African-Canadian women — many of them immigrants from the Caribbean — also entered the job market. Some had left their children, male partners and husbands back in the Caribbean with the expectation that these family members would join them later. Many of these women were able to gain entry to Canada as domestic workers during the 1960s and 1970s because they were single.[10]

To fully understand the lives of single mothers and their sons (see Fraser 2011), we must pay attention to their multiple located histories and multi-layered relationships to the socio-economic conditions of the community in which they reside, and the opportunities that are afforded them — all of which are mediated by expectations and perceptions of them by the larger society. According to Nancy Dowd (1997: 3),

> a remarkably consistent view of single-parent families dominates popular culture as well as public policy. "Single-parent family" is a euphemism... for "problem family," for some kind of social pathology.... Single-parent families are characterized as part of the "underclass"; broken and deviant, as compared to the nuclear, traditional, patriarchal family. Some equate the rise in the numbers of single-parent families with social decline and the death of the "real" family.

Evidently, the dysfunctions and social pathologies of single mothers and their fatherless sons are not of their own making. We are quite acquainted with the mothers (many of them minorities and/or immigrants) who sometimes, despite their level of education, work at minimum wage jobs and must work many hours — often at multiple jobs — to support their families. Daycare and babysitters are expensive and in many cases are inaccessible. Frequently, children babysat by television and youth left to their own devices can become vulnerable to undesired influences despite their parents' attempts to positively influence them. There are cases in which teachers appeal to mothers about their sons' repeated absence from school, their disruptive behaviours and their low grades, only to be appealed to in return by anxious and worn-out mothers who are at a loss as to how to keep their sons on the right path — in school and out of trouble. Teachers and parents share the same desires but neither is powerful enough alone, or even together, to fight the cruelty of poverty, limited family and social supports, an alienating school system and a discriminating society. Therefore, even as single mothers employ their "parent-centred approach" to parent their sons — an approach that in many cases is based on their own experiences growing up — it seems not to work. In fact, an authoritarian, restrictive and punitive parenting style is seen as insensitive to children's needs because of its demand for complete obedience. Researchers suggest that children raised in this way are unlikely to do as well in school as their White peers (see Ginwright 2007; Gosa and Alexander 2007).

We do not suggest that a child should not have the benefit of two caring parents. Rather our attempt here is to draw attention to the limits of the singular and simplistic approach to assessing the disengagement of Black boys from their schooling and their involvement in damaging activities. It is not sufficient to simply refer to the fact that Black students, compared to their peers, were more likely to live with one parent, usually their mother.[11] Additional information is needed to explain how history, economics, and social policies and supports[12] operate in shaping and reshaping family structures, thereby helping to produce the young men that boys become. It is quite limiting for conversations about the situation of Black young men to focus so extensively on single mothers, absent fathers and their moral failings. Is doing so an attempt to address an inherent problem of our society? Or is it, as some community activist claim, a play on old racial, sexualizing stereotypes of Black people as promiscuous and careless? Questions aside, the fact remains, marginalized boys — and Black boys in particular — are disproportionately disengaged from school, academically underachieving, dropping out and entering the justice system.[13] One of the responses to this situation has been to offer mentoring and special schooling programs for boys, and to establish schooling for Black students. We examine these further "fixes" in the following sections.

Mentoring and Role Modelling:
Counteracting the Underachievement of Boys

An underlying assumption fuels the call for mentors and role models. It is based on the notion that the lack of a father figure for young Black men means that they have not learned about maleness from those best suited to teach them, and so have gone, or will eventually go, "astray." This cultural or essentialist argument places the responsibility for the issues and problems directly on the youth, their families and the community, leaving unexamined and unaddressed the socio-historical, systemic or structural factors that account for the situation in the first place. It is understandable, then, with the focus on the failings of young men and their parents, that role models and mentors would be called upon to "fix" the problem.

While mentorship and role modelling might be reasonable approaches to the social challenges some boys face,[14] providing them with mentors or placing men in teaching positions to become role models might not yield the expected results. In fact, such a move could aggravate existing difficulties. Sevier and Ashcraft (2007) question how the incorporation of male teachers without a constructionist gender analysis can address the perceived need for more male role models. They argue that an automated "surrogate-father" rationale

> does not articulate or even question what masculinity is or what kinds of masculinities we wish to model. Furthermore it presumes that boys are much more likely to imitate and admire male teachers rather than female teachers. This simplistic (sex-role socialization) assumption suggests that only girls can imitate women or that women cannot communicate models of positive masculine behavior to boys. (536)

Sevier and Ashcroft go on to critique the premise of sex-role socialization that is used to promote male teachers for male students.

> Although male teachers are important and further bring unique insights to the profession, an overemphasis on women's limitations in this area minimizes the positive effects that women can have on the socialization of young boys. Reinforcing this problem, researchers and educators typically stress that this is especially significant in light of the rising number of single-parent households. This justification comes close to suggesting that the presence of men is a necessary corrective to the damaging affects of over-exposure to single mothers or other women. (536)

Obviously, the essentialist assumptions of sex-role mentorships can have unforeseen consequences, especially in cases in which mentors are not fully able to relate to the life circumstances of their mentees, or do not have a full grasp of the mentees' social situation. For even though mentors might claim to have come from similar life circumstances and have now "made it," the message to their mentees that "I have made it, therefore you can too" could be more a liability or hindrance than the needed encouragement. Furthermore, notwithstanding the constructive impact that male mentors can and do have on mentees, promoting the idea that men can learn only from men could unintentionally serve to undermine the support, relevance and credibility of female parents, caregivers and teachers, and as a consequence, discipline problems and conflicts can arise. If the benefits of the role model and mentor are to be maximized, then those who present themselves as such need to actively and consistently engage, if not personify, an intentional critique of gender and gender construction, offer clarity around issues of gender identity and performance and make every effort not to re-inscribe the patriarchal ethos of masculinity performance. Ironically, this is a process that would diminish the need for sex-specific mentoring. However, Sevier and Ashcraft indicate that this practice does not happen in most role-modelling relationships. They assert that while male teachers may "embrace the idea that they should act as male role models, they struggle to articulate what that means" (2007: 3). This kind of self-reflection and practice is even more crucial in gender-based or single-sex educational settings.

Indeed, if in their roles as mentors and role models, teachers are to effectively support students to operate in a world where there is equity and equality among the sexes, then they have to critically reflect and disclose their position on what it means for males and females to learn differently. How will they work with claims, such as those mentioned in a *Globe and Mail* article?

> Boys need to move while girls have the ability to sit still and work. Boys thrive on team competition and relish a battle against a buddy, while girls would rather be on the same team. Boys tend not to look at the teacher as a friend or ally, while girls do. Boys tend to be bored by context, while girls tend to appreciate context. Boys tend to need feedback immediately, while girls can wait for a day or two for feedback. In completing tasks, boys are more likely to be satisfied with getting started, while girls like to see beginning, middle and the end. (Boesveld 2010)

An important question that must be answered here is, which boys? And if these differences are "real," how do we respond to their differentiated needs and interests when they are in the same or separate classrooms? How do we recognize and respond to these differences (if we decide that they are "real") without becoming complicit in perpetuating them?

In the absence of acknowledging the heterogeneity among boys — in terms of race, ethnicity, sexuality, religion, athletic ability and aptitude, interests, aspirations and so forth — mentors and role models are likely (sometimes unwittingly in the context of a patriarchal school culture) to contribute to the socially constructed differences that we claim exist among males and females. Beyond accepting these differences as a given, we need to reflect on how we help to create and maintain these perceived differences even as we claim to be advocates for equity and equality in our institutions and society generally. One of the barriers to changing the discourse is the cultural or biological principle that is so readily taken up — that the differences are "natural" or "inborn," rather than constructed psycho-social responses — and therefore contributing to the gendered performance of individuals. Naming boys' disengagement from school, their low levels of achievement or their anti-academic/protest behaviours as primarily cultural would prove to be unproductive in responding to their needs and interests. In the context of fatherlessness and sex-specific role-modelling debates, the supposed fundamental sex differences all but necessitate other males to manage and motivate unruly boys.

While some good does come from mentorship and role modelling, it should not act as a substitute for an engagement of the complex systemic and structural issues that shape social relationships, personal decisions and individuals' outcomes (see also Martino and Rezai-Rashti 2010; McCready 2010; Rezai-Rashti and Martino 2010). Clearly, the practice is far from reliable and the intended outcomes are not guaranteed. For instance, Jordan Manners had access to male mentors and role models. But did they, in his mind, understand his needs, encourage his interests and satisfy his aspirations? We will never know. But we do know of Jordan's involvement with the Youth Association for Academics, Athletics and Character Education (YAAACE) program run by Devon Jones and Devon Thompson. In fact, I (Carl) met Jordan in the spring of 2006, one year before the shooting, when Mr. Jones, his teacher, brought him and seven other Grade 8 students on a tour of the university. I remember meeting Jordon in the Faculty of Education as he curiously surveyed his surroundings. By coincidence, on the evening of the shooting, having waited for some time for Mr. Jones to go downtown,[15] I called him. Upon answering my call, Mr. Jones, in a voice full of anguish, said: "One of my boys was killed this afternoon." The anguish indicated a feeling of resignation that, despite his efforts, he had been unable to prevent Jordan's early demise. Evidently, there is a limit to what we can expect from the efforts of mentors and role models. Their work must be complemented, not only by that of parents, but also by teachers, principals, police and other socializing agents.

Africentric Schooling: From Idea to Realization

After the sorrow and grieving, the self-reflection, the search for explanations to the unimaginable incident inside a school and the call for something to be done to address the worrying educational problems affecting Black youth, we expected a substantial endorsement by Torontonians for something — anything — that would be responsive to the needs, interests, expectations and aspirations of Black youth and their parents. But when the Toronto District School Board proposed introducing an Africentric alternative school — long put forward by community members[16] as a course of action — the idea evoked mixed reactions. After a bitter debate, the Board of Trustees voted eleven to nine in favour of instituting an Africentric school. The Ontario premier indicated his disapproval, saying he regretted that he could do nothing to stop the school and asserted: "I don't think it's a good idea. I'm not personally comfortable with that.... I think our shared responsibility... is to look for ways to bring people together... through publicly funded education" (Rushowy 2007). The opposition leader also condemned the move, as did the Minister of Education, who stated, "We don't think the board should be moving in this direction" (*Toronto Star* 2008). Media reports and commentaries branded the idea of instituting an Africentric school as "segregationist." The *Toronto Star* claimed that "the idea smacks of segregation, which is contrary to the values of the school system and Canadian society as a whole." The *Globe and Mail* described the recommendations "as insulting as they are ridiculous"; and the *National Post* suggested that "the concept of special schools for black students is one of those terrible ideas that refuse to die" (see Wallace 2009: 4).

Indeed, having a Black-focused, Afrocentric or Africentric school is an idea that "refuses to die." Since the 1980s, given the consistent research evidence that indicates Black youth are underachieving and dropping out of school, parents and community members have been demanding educational programs that speak directly to the needs and concerns of Black students (James 1996).[17] To this end, Stephen Lewis and later the Four-level Government/African Canadian Community Working Group (who were commissioned after the "Yonge Street riots"[18] in 1992 to report on the problems that might have precipitated them) gave support to the idea of having a Black-focused school. Referring to a number of reports and presentations, the Working Group wrote that "for at least one generation, the African-Canadian community has been crying out in anguish over the poor performance of its youth in the Ontario School system" (*Towards a New Beginning* 1992: 77). Two years later, the Royal Commission on Learning, established by the Ontario government in 1993 to study the educational needs of students, reported that Black students, parents and community leaders expressed "serious concerns" about the level of educational achievement of their students and "frustration over lack of improvement over the years, during which time they have voiced their concerns to school boards and to the Ministry" (Begin and Caplan 1994: 439–431). The Commission went on to recommend that, in areas with large numbers of Black students, "innovative strategies" be used and "special programmes" be established that would address the "urgent need to substantially improve the academic performance of Black students" (433).[19]

By 2006, the Toronto District School Board signalled its willingness to address the disengagement, poor performance and high drop-out rates of Black students as indicated by its research. That year trustee Stephnie Payne (who represented the Jane and Finch area) initiated and chaired a committee[20] made up of community members, teachers, administrators and other board personnel to prepare a plan for a school (not just a program) that would be responsive to the schooling needs of underachieving students — in short, an Africentric school. Furthermore, the shooting incident and findings from two reports — one commissioned by the school board (Julian Falconer, Peggy Edwards and Linda MacKinnon) and the other by the Ontario government (Roy McMurtry and Alvin Curling) — pointed to the need to address the sense of hopelessness and violence we were witnessing among young people. Falconer, Edwards and MacKinnon (2008: 6) noted that the focus on zero tolerance and related disciplinary measures in schools was failing to decrease the level of violence among young people, and as such, "hope needs to be restored through programs and initiatives that create prospects for success for young people who are currently on the outside looking in." McMurtry and Curling (2008: 141) wrote that the hopelessness and violence tended to be among young people — especially minority young people — residing in neighbourhoods characterized by higher concentration of poverty, structural manifestation of racism, family breakdown and lack of both adequate public spaces for gathering and recreation. They suggested that "limited resources must be put where they will have the biggest impact on the roots of violence involving youth."

Despite the findings of the commissioned reports, the expansive research, the shooting incidents and the years-long call for educational reforms to address the schooling situation of Black youth, public sentiment continued to be against establishing a school that would address these needs and concerns. Even as the Africentric elementary school has demonstrated its usefulness, there is still a reluctance to cater to the educational needs of a population of students who can benefit from a different kind of educational program. This objection to the elementary Africentric Alternative School established in 2009, which seemingly had been simmering for the two years of its existence, found expression when the Toronto District School Board announced its proposal to establish an Africentric Secondary School in September 2011. The reason for people's "outrage" (as the media framed it) — that of students, teachers, parents, board trustees, editorial writers — was because the Toronto District School Board had "failed to consult students, teachers and the surrounding community" of the school where the Africentric school would be housed (Vaccaro 2011).[21] At a hastily called community meeting following the media report, some 400 people went to the proposed school to protest. According to *Toronto Star* reporter Louise Brown (2011b), who had been writing of the Africentric elementary school,

Students, graduates, parents and members of the black community packed the auditorium of the historic high school on St. Clair Ave. to discuss a staff proposal to open the alternative school in a bid to tackle a 40-per-cent drop out rate among Toronto's black students. However most of the audience opposed the idea… calling it segregation and warning it would divide a school that is already highly diverse. Emotions have run so high since media reports of the proposal last weekend, that at least six police officers attended the meeting as a precaution after the school received several threats Tuesday.

Students at the school were said to have organized a Facebook petition opposing the initiative. Eventually, as the headline of Brown's article reads, the "plan for the Africentric high school [was] put on hold amid packed and angry protest."

Why the outrage and anger in response to the establishing of the school? Why the reluctance to try — just *try* — something different, since what has been tried to date seems not to be working? After all, conventional wisdom is that in addressing a problem (or in researching a problem), one should try as many approaches (or go at the problem from as many angles) as possible to achieve the required results — particularly when simple or minor adjustments to existing programs have not helped. Hence, an Africentric Secondary School seems logical, particularly if we take into account that

> certain groups in our society are treated inequitably because of individual and systemic biases related to race, colour, culture, ethnicity, linguistic origin, disability, socio-economic class, age, ancestry, nationality, place of origin, religion, faith, sex, gender, sexual orientation, family status, and marital status. We also acknowledge that such biases exist within our school system. (Toronto District School Board 2000)

Besides, it is generally accepted that individuals learn in diverse and varying ways and contexts. As such, it is inconsiderate to stifle educational options or a school board's willingness to be responsive to the learning needs and styles of students. On this basis, therefore, an Africentric Secondary School — just like the many other specialty or alternative programs and schools in Ontario and within the Toronto District School Board[22] — is merited and would be fulfilling a need. But even after the public meetings in the fall of 2008, and the evidence provided by the elementary Africentric Alternative School since September 2009, the public discourse maintains that such a school represents a step backward to the days of segregation — something against which Martin Luther King fought. Such a claim devalues the important difference between regulated segregation and a group's decision regarding the educational, cultural and social approaches — including exclusive grouping if necessary — that can best prepare them to not only meet the needs of their community, but also for community members to gain what it takes to meaningfully participate in society. Why would immigrant parents and grandparents want it otherwise, given that they emigrated to make a better life for themselves and their offspring?

The perception that Black students would go en masse from the mainstream school system into the "Blacks-only" school fuelled a fear that the door to a full-scale system of separate schools for Blacks and other non-White students would be opened up. The public discourse served to polarize rather than to educate. It was deeply irrational, and feigning objectivity and logic, people purposely and strategically ignored simple facts and recent history. Jordan Manners' mother — now a media "go to" parent on schooling issues — came out against the school. Essentially, the anger and irrational reasoning that fuelled the consistent objections to the school suggest that more was at stake than just the fate of a few Black kids. What was at stake was the preservation of the Canadian identity and the dream of multiculturalism, which is to say that Canadians are living, learning, working and playing harmoniously together. So a "Blacks-only" school, as it was referred to even in the media, was un-Canadian. In fact, allowing Africentric schooling would mean conceding that "race matters in Canada and therefore plays a role in the experiences of Black students" (James 2011: 4; see also James 2010).

The difficult birth of the Africentric Alternative School in September of 2009 was significant for two reasons. First, the school itself would be able to provide useful insights into how to best meet the needs of Black students and support them in their learning. While this one school will help those who attend it, it is ultimately the mainstream school system that must change to resolve the problem of Black students' disengagement and underachievement. For this school to be of value to Black students throughout the TDSB, what is learned there must be shared with the entire school system. While many in the Black community support the Africentric program, there are more who would prefer that Black students be served by an effective mainstream system. Evidently, a parallel school system for all Black students is neither feasible nor desirable. Yet, despite a provincial curriculum that suggests a capacity to be inclusive of all students, most classrooms remain Eurocentric and non-inclusive, and this is affecting the educational performance of Black students. The controversy surrounding Africentric schooling has helped to focus attention on how the educational system has failed them, but it was Manners' murder that demonstrated that this issue is no longer only about equity, class, race or social justice, but about life and death.

Conclusion

Jordon Manners' shooting did what the killing of a young person often does — it made us want to do something. But, soon after the initial shock, the appropriate grace period and our preliminary answers to the niggling, predictable questions, we seem to return to business as usual. It should not take the death of an innocent youth for us to pay attention to their schooling and social situation; for social activists to hustle funding for programs and schooling for which they will have to fight every year to maintain; or for us to make the necessary systemic changes that provide youth with a sense of hope, purpose and possibilities. That a student had to be killed and an "independent" investigation held should be a signal that the institutions responsible for the care and socialization of our young people are failing them, and that individuals charged with these tasks have little understanding of their needs, issues and problems. Manners' death should not obfuscate the larger societal problems that contributed to his murder.

At a public consultation held by the panel appointed by the school board to investigate school safety, one young community member commented that "Jordan Manners didn't die because of the school. He died because of the streets" (Marlow 2007). This comment rightly stresses that the problem is not merely about schooling or schools, but rather about community and about society. It is also about the role of the media in promoting the status quo discourse. How the community is positioned by the larger society affects the school. If the students in the school are considered to be "at risk," that has some relationship to the school and the community in which the students live. This dynamic between the student, school, community and society indicates that ultimately we are all implicated in the outcomes of our youth — some institutions and people more than others. While schools are said to be instruments against society's inequities and oppressions, they nevertheless mirror and re-inscribe these structures. In fact, claims that schools operate on a system of meritocracy cannot be sustained. Contradictions to this claim are evidenced by their failure to provide students living in marginalized communities with the needed critical understanding of their lives, an understanding that would enable them to access the promised social and educational opportunities in society.

Focusing on fatherlessness, mentorship, policing and gun control allows us as a society to feel that something can be done about the sense of hopelessness, violence and crime among our youth. Focusing on poor single mothers conveys the idea that if they just followed society's sexual mores or rules, much of the trouble with their children would be avoided. The discourse lets us turn away from the systemic issues that produce children who disengage from school and are kept outside of mainstream society. This misdirection is a disservice, for it focuses on the individual youth and their parents and not on the social context that plays a role in producing the youth that she or he becomes. What a youth becomes is as much a reflection of the youth's position — or understanding of his or her position — in society, and the sense of belonging and purpose that is communicated to that youth.

Evidently, there is a need for real change. This requires radical shifts in the social structures and in our thinking about race, class, poverty, youth and parenting. Schools should be at the forefront of such change. These kind of radical shifts, however, are easy to call for and difficult to implement. So do we continue to call for it, knowing the futility of that call? Do we continue to tell ourselves that dual families, "positive" role models, mentorship programs, religious conversions, community soul-searching and "more respect for and cooperation with authorities such as police and teachers" (O'Grady, Parnaby and Schikschneit 2010: 70) will create the change that is necessary? Maybe reforms are pipe dreams, but demanding it requires truth-telling, and truth-telling can be the beginning of change. It would be good not to have underachieving students, violent incidents and funerals in which the blame is placed on beleaguered parents and communities while the rest of the society is exonerated. There should be no more young boys whose shattered dreams to be rappers or basketball stars demonstrate the narrowness of the horizons given or communicated to them (no matter how many journalists suggest otherwise). We can begin with schools and reclaim the faded notion of education as social change, ensuring that commitment to equity in education is real and concerned with social justice.

The CBC's *Fifth Estate* (2007) presented the documentary "Lost in the Struggle," which followed three young men from Jane and Finch, chronicling their fight to create a space for themselves in the world even as they tried to escape a life of crime and police encounters. A fourth subject, it is said, was edited out of the documentary because of time constraints. That boy was Jordan Manners.

Notes

1. This chapter was written with the assistance of Adrian Worrell.
2. The two young men pleaded "not guilty" to the charges. In March 2010, after the jury was unable to reach a verdict, a mistrial was declared. They were again tried

in the spring of 2011 and found not guilty of murder in May 2011. The Crown did not appeal. According to one news report, the Crown Attorney "admitted one of the missing pieces" in the case was a motive — the boys were "Jordan's friends, and there was no suggestion of any animus." The defence was that Jordan was accidentally shot (O'Toole 2011).

3.   O'Grady, Parnaby and Schikschneit (2010: 56) also make the point that "although the media initially sought to contextualize Manners' death by referring to previous school shootings... within approximately 48 hours, a very different, dominant framework appeared, one that framed the killing as if it were a tragedy that had its roots in the very nature of Toronto's black, urban 'underclass.'"

4.   Of course, there were the conversations and news reports that talked of Manners and others as the "special needs" or "at-risk" students they were labelled or perceived to be (see Marlow 2007; DiManno 2010).

5.   While the media did report that some relatives were "known to police," friends, family and even school officials knew that it was essential that they assert that Manners was not involved in any gang-related activity. This was essential if public support and certainly sympathy were to be maintained.

6.   Interestingly, O'Grady, Parnaby and Schikschneit (2010: 69) observed from their review of media reports of the shooting that the media did not present any comments from experts about "the possible cause of the shooting" as is typical in the reporting of such incidents. The only comments were from grief counsellors about "how students in a state of shock could best recover from the experience." The authors conclude that the media reports were largely "grounded in pre-existing typologies" of the community as violent and in doing so conflated "stereotypical notions of race (black), gender (male), and socio-economic status (low)." The "common-sense" explanation is that such an incident is what can be expected from such a community.

7.   In their chapter, "Governing the Young," Ericson and Haggerty (1999: 163) equate these risk classifications to a form of governance. They write that "governance is organized in terms of risk management technologies" that serve to sort "people into population categories that identify who is at risk and who poses risk." Increasingly, surveillance of young people remains one of the bases on which they are managed.

8.   Ericson and Haggerty (1999: 164) write that through "school-based programmes, police officers function simultaneously as security educators, informant system operators, counsellors and gatekeepers for special programmes that deal with youth at risk."

9.   The 2001 Census data indicate that 46 percent of African-Canadian children ages fourteen and under (compared to a national average of 18 percent) are growing up in one-parent, typically single-mother households (Milan and Tran 2004: 5).

10.   There were cases of Caribbean women being deported because they lied on their immigration application. They did not declare that they had children. Others had a very difficult time bringing their children to Canada because they too did not admit to having children that they had left behind. Further, the years of separation from spouse and children evidently contributed to the number of family break-ups that occurred.

11.   In their final report on school safety, Falconer, Edwards and MacKinnon (2008) note that 38 percent of Black students surveyed lived with both parents, whereas

84 percent of West Asian students, 83 percent of South Asian students and 77 percent of Asian students did.

12. Falconer and his colleagues (2008) also reported that 6 percent of South Asians, 11 percent of West Asians and 12 percent of Asians stated that they lived in social housing, compared to 35 percent of Black students.

13. See McKell (2010): "Achievement Gap Task Force: Draft Report"; Bhattacharjee (2003): *The Ontario Safe Schools Act: School Discipline and Discrimination*; James and Taylor (2010): "The Making of At Risk Students"; Daniel and Bondy (2008): "Safe Schools and Zero Tolerance: Policy, Program and Practice in Ontario."

14. Ramon San Vicente (2011: 11) asserts that "mentorship also offers a means of professional development for educators that can be unparalleled in its ability to provide insight into what works for most marginalized student populations and for all students." He goes on to say that it became "a transformational opportunity for me to refine my pedagogical practice, challenge destructive versions of masculinity, build relationships with parents and community, engage in curriculum that was culturally relevant and grounded in a more nuanced understanding of the lives of my mentees all within an approach that was less traditional and more responsive."

15. Mr. Jones, ten of Jordan's peers from the community — some of them former classmates and friends — and I went to a restaurant downtown for dinner with Johnny Williams, a former basketball player from Detroit, who, on occasion, would sponsor activities for the youth in the YAAACE program. Interestingly, in the hour it took us to get downtown in the limousine, the youth's attention was affixed to the television screen that was carrying live reports of the shooting. During the two hours we spent at dinner, the youth said nothing about the incident; neither did they give more than one-word responses to my questions about whether they knew Jordan, and when they last saw him. They admitted to knowing about the shooting only from the media. The stunned silence around the incident indicated to me that these youth were trying to understand it all and were in a state of emotional unease, not knowing quite how to process it.

16. In 2007, the TDSB Alternative Schools Advisory Committee, based on representation from two parents, approved the establishment of the school as it does with all other alternative school requests.

17. In fact, in September 1986, under the leadership of Jackie Wilson and with the assistance of Veronica Sullivan and Afua Cooper, the Afro-Caribbean Alternative Secondary School was established with forty-five students, ages sixteen years and older, and a small number of qualified teachers. Initially the school had three classrooms in a school in the former City of York. After a year, the school was reduced to a program and lasted only eighteen months (Wallace 2009: 3).

18. The so-called Yonge Street riots occurred after a demonstration in downtown Toronto, partly in response to a police shooting of a young Black man in the city in the week following the Rodney King beating verdict and subsequent L.A. riots.

19. In 1995, a Black-focused school program, N'ghana, for high-school students was established within the former Toronto Board of Education. The program, which initially operated in a community centre staffed by qualified teachers, was moved from one school to another and in the process lost the support needed for it to continue. Today there is hardly any reference to the fact that the program existed.

20. Through this committee a number of Africentric summer programs and curriculum projects were initiated and implemented in schools in the Jane-Finch

area — an area where there is a significant number of Black students with a disproportionately low level of educational achievement. In the end, Sheppard Public School, located just outside of Jane and Finch, was chosen to house the Africentric Alternative School. The school was opened in September 2009 with well over 100 students enrolled in kindergarten to Grade 5. A grade has been added each year, resulting in well over 170 students attending the school by the fall of 2011. It is expected that the school will offer kindergarten to Grade 8 by 2012.

21. It should be noted that the proposed school for the Africentric school (a school inside the school) had the capacity to house another 300 students.

22. For instance, there are religious schools (including Catholic schools), girls' and boys' schools, Aboriginal and French schools, and schools that focus on social justice, arts, athletics and environment.

Chapter 6

Beyond the Intersection
Toward a Community-Centred Approach to Schooling

By way of concluding this text, I draw on the reflections of Kulsoom Anwer and Samuel (Sam) Tecle, two young adults who grew up in the neighbourhood and whose stories demonstrate the significant role that the community has played in their lives and schooling. Their varied histories and complex relationships with the community provide insights, not only to Kulsoom and Sam as individuals, but also to the many young people who live, learn, play and work in the community. And as Sam often emphasizes, "in spite of" or "despite" the stereotyping and problems they encountered, they managed to attain the educational and occupational goals to which they aspired. Given what we hear from young people who are committed to making a difference and "giving back" to their community, it should not be surprising that both Kulsoom and Sam have become teachers and endeavour to use their skills and knowledge in the service of their community. Critical to an appreciation of their contribution to this discussion is enabling Kulsoom and Sam to share their stories in their own words, from start to finish. In this way, we will be able to see their thinking, note how they analyze their experiences and witness how they broke out of the bounded and limited ways they had imagined their worlds, constructed their aspirations and maintained a sense of optimism.

As racialized youth with immigrant parents, both Kulsoom and Sam represent how youth of their generation negotiated and navigated the cultural, social and educational structures in their bid to attain their aspirations, which, by their own admission, were constructed in relation to their parents' class and migrant mobility dreams — dreams premised on the belief that it is through education that their children will succeed in Canadian society (see also Chapter 4).

"More Than an Intersection"
Kulsoom Anwer
Like many Canadian immigrants, my parents began their married life together in an apartment building, not too far from the Jane-Finch intersection in Toronto. My father had emigrated from Pakistan in the sixties. He returned to get married in the seventies; my mother joined him in Toronto

soon after. My brother and I were both born in the hospital right across from the high school we would attend years later, Westview Centennial. When I was about three years old and my parents were ready to buy a house, they looked all over the city, but also in Jane and Finch. They were aware of the reputation the area had, but having lived there, could see beyond it. My mother liked its pedestrian-friendly layout and liveliness, but most of all, its multiculturalism. She often told us when we were growing up that she hadn't wanted to move to an area where the neighbourhood kids wouldn't play with us because of the colour of our skin. She didn't want us to grow up battling racism, feeling different, struggling for acceptance; in this area, so humbled by the media's characterizations and its own very real challenges, she saw the possibility of a different Canada, where the children of immigrants were not a minority. Where darker skin was no cause for note and everyone came from somewhere away.

The wisdom of this philosophy struck me very early. I have always felt at home in Jane and Finch. I went to Topcliff Elementary, Oakdale Park M.S. and Westview Centennial S.S. At every school transition, everyone around me would talk about other schools they could go to — no one's parents wanted them to go to Oakdale, and later to Westview. The reputations of these schools preceded them. Instead they looked to schools close, but less close, Elia Middle School and C.W. Jefferys. In the end, it usually proved impossible for most to get into schools outside of their attendance area. But at my house, there was no such talk. My mom told us that our school experience would be what we made it. We made it a good one. In fact, I liked my neighbourhood, my peers and our schools so much I decided to become a teacher. I returned to Westview in 2002 as a student teacher. When I graduated from York University I tried to get a job teaching there. When none was available, I took one teaching at Sir Sandford Fleming Academy in the Lawrence Heights neighbourhood. This area, known as the "Jungle," has the same challenges as Jane and Finch, beginning with a social housing stigma.

My schooling experience in Jane and Finch was positive because I felt like I belonged. I was surrounded by students who shared immigrant parents and class background. But my experience was singular too. I came to school with the middle-class literacy practices my mother brought over from her life in Pakistan, which ensured I would be successful in this system. I was always in the "advanced" stream, now known as "academic," which meant the world of schooling I lived in at Jane and Finch was somewhat sheltered. Even so, I knew that many of my peers were not successful in school, those in the "advanced" stream as well as not; this informed my interest in teaching. I knew these kids—they were me. Why weren't more of us going to university? Of those of us who did go, why didn't all of us stay? These were only a couple of the questions I had growing up in Jane and Finch. The rest are raised throughout this book.

This year, I return to the area to teach English. I am not alone. I know so many of my peers who have become teachers and returned to the area to "give back." Some never left. That so many of us became teachers speaks to the quality of commitment of many of the teachers we had. And yet, we return to do things differently. When I went to high school, I never heard the words "colonialism" or "post-colonialism"; only a couple of teachers mentioned anti-racism. My students, and not just my "academic" students, know these words. They know what stigma is, what cultural capital is, what code-switching is. They know where I come from and where I am now. Like all teachers, I am the first piece of curriculum in my classroom. Growing up in Jane and Finch has given me my "teaching heart," and I think, *particularly* in urban areas, your heart comes first. But it is not enough to care about your students. I think almost every teacher does. My teaching heart wants for them what I want for myself, what I want for my daughter. Jane and Finch is where they live; it is their story and it is mine.

Samuel (Sam) Tecle
For my parents, Canada represented a place of refuge and escape from a difficult and uncertain life in a territory (Eritrea) in the midst of a struggle for liberation — a gamble of sorts. With me — their two-year-old son, they landed in Vancouver and then moved to Toronto. We eventually settled in Jane and Finch when I was five years old. It was in the early 1990s when we took up residence in a highrise building in the Tobermory neighbourhood (T-Block), located one block east of the Jane and Finch intersection. This is one of the many neighbourhoods that make up the Jane-Finch community.

These neighbourhoods co-exist and are concurrently held captive by the dominant narrative of the urban ghetto that Jane and Finch has come to represent. The singularity and simplicity of the dominant narrative has become a burden assumed by many residents of the community — whether willingly or not. I remember many meetings on the first floor of our building of concerned residents, community workers and activists worried about the dominant narrative — often in sensationalized media reports — that portrayed our community as populated by mostly Black people and ravaged by violence and poverty. I also remember many saying at these meetings that they had the choice to leave the community many years ago, but chose to stay. Often these discussions grew into community action on how to challenge the overbearing single perception of the community.

Living in a community that is overly represented by a negative story meant learning to push back against the alluring simplicity of the dominant narrative or perception. In time, the portrayal of your community becomes very much a part of who you are and what you do that you can never really escape. Whether you reject, accept or choose to ignore the dominant narrative, in a way it is still a part of your story. So a large part of growing up in Jane and Finch meant that you inevitably inherit this struggle for fair, equal and balanced representation. As a community, we may be separate on the basis of neighbourhoods or geography, but we band together when our community (of neighbourhoods) — our "home" — is under attack.

I remember having to do the bulk of the work of defending my community at the middle and high schools I attended. The middle school I went to was located ten miles due east from Jane and Finch in an area of the city that was foreign to me. For a Jane and Finch boy at age thirteen, taking the 36 Finch West bus all the way to school and leaving everything and everyone I knew was not easy. But according to my parents and teachers, it was "necessary." As many of my teachers identified based on my excellent grades, I had "potential" that they felt would best be realized if I was away from the company I was keeping. What is important to observe here is that my parents were working class, and from their perspective, it was either permitting their son with "potential" to attain the education he needed or letting him fall to the thralls of the community. Hence, after a few different primary schools, my desperate parents and very well-meaning teachers, with help from a caring principal, decided that it would be best to have me start middle school outside of the Jane-Finch community. Perhaps they too were operating from the deficit or limitation model, and concluded that removing me from the community was an (the) answer to the perplexing contradiction that was me — a high-achieving student with less than desirable behaviour; it must be the fault of the community.

The environment surrounding my middle school was considerably different from anything I was familiar with "back home." The school was located in a middle-class neighbourhood, and judging by the size of some of the two-car-garage homes in the area, I assumed that they were well above middle class. The students were predominantly White and I was one of the very few Black students — the only one, during my years there, enrolled in the enriched track at the school. Adjusting to the starkly different demographics was not as easy as the academics were. However, I excelled at the school — a school with a "very good reputation," I kept hearing. That was never said about the schools in Jane and Finch, yet I had excelled there as well. My classmates and teachers alike were aware of the fact that I was from Jane and Finch and was a "special" student. This precarious status was perhaps confirmed by the personal interest the principal had taken in me. What I represented was the embodiment of the "Other" — Black, poor and from Jane and Finch. These distinctions became synonymous and superfluous. It was difficult going to any social gatherings. The reasons for this were twofold: I rarely got invited, and I lived almost a world away.

There was one incident I vividly recall in Grade 7 in which I felt particularly tokenized. The unit we were working on was Speech Writing, and this unit consisted of writing a speech and then presenting it to the class. I had written a speech on living in Jane and Finch, perhaps in response to the never-ending daily questions from students as well as from some staff pertaining to "what it was really like to live there." The speech lasted four minutes and thirty seconds and was well written and emotionally charged. I implicated my classmates as well as some teachers in explaining how assumptions and the dominating negative perceptions can make a person feel helpless. I remember feeling some trepidation about whether or not I should actually read the speech and wondered how it would make my classmates and teacher feel. I read the speech and will never forget the dead moment of silence right after, and the silence being broken by a single clap that was followed by more applause.

The speech began to make waves throughout the school. Teachers heard about it as did other students from all three grades. Each class voted on which speech was going to represent them at the school-wide speech contest, and according to my Language Arts teacher, the votes for mine were unanimous. Even the other finalists voted for my speech to represent our class at the school-wide competition. Although it was a great honour to be chosen to represent our class, I remember feeling quite nervous about giving the speech to the whole school. After the school-wide competition, the best three speeches would go on to compete at the district competition. In the days leading up to the competition, I heard that most of the student body was going to vote for my speech. I remember deeply questioning what this meant. Why did everyone want to hear my speech? I wondered about the impact it had had on the students in my class and on my Language Arts teacher, and what they were telling others about it. I dismissed the fears as stage fright and went on to give the speech to the whole school. It was again well received. I did, in fact, go on to represent Grade 7 at the district competition. Yet, while mixed with feelings of accomplishment and pride, the fears and doubts lingered. I wondered why my fellow students and teachers had such an enduring interest in a community they had never stepped in and knew only through news reports and troubling articles.

I attended the high school in the area into which my middle school feeds. There my academic accomplishments continued. I received both academic and athletic accolades, as well as a diploma in both French and

English. All this, while feeling ambivalent about having to leave my community for schooling. What did that say about Jane and Finch — about how my family, teachers and I felt about the community — that we could live here but not be schooled here? But in leaving the security of my home community, I had set out on the path toward fulfilling the immigrant dreams and hopes of my family and most Eritreans. For them, it was directly through education that middle-class life was to be achieved. It is understandable, then, that my siblings were expected to, and did, follow the same educational path.

After high school, I enrolled in the Kinesiology and Health Sciences Program at York University, which is located about two and a half blocks northeast of our apartment. I chose York over the three other universities to which I had applied and received acceptance because, to me, it meant attending school in my community. As a result, when my parents were able to purchase our first house after nearly twenty years of living in the community, and considered moving to Brampton (some twenty miles away) like many of the residents from the building, I was against it. (In fact, other communities such as Scarborough and Brampton seemed like abstract places on a map somewhere, a map I had never seen and had no interest in exploring.) I used accessibility to the university and my position as the oldest child — as much as etiquette and tradition would allow — to persuade my parents to stay in the area, keeping in mind that this was their dream and that they had made many sacrifices to get to this point. My parents did purchase a house about three blocks south of our apartment building. To my parents, this means that they are now living outside of Jane and Finch. Nevertheless, I continue to believe that I reside in the community. So when I chose to pursue teacher education, I decided on the Urban Diversity Program at York University, which by happenstance is housed right in the centre of Jane and Finch.

Beyond personal connections and schooling, I also worked in the community, from running basketball leagues at the local recreation centre to creating and co-facilitating a hip-hop literacy program called Spoken N' Heard. I also worked at the Jane and Finch Boys and Girls Club one summer and even at the hospital as a security guard. After qualifying as a teacher I taught for two summers in a summer program for Grade 8 students entering the local high schools who needed the credits necessary for high school.

My story is a story among many stories that tend to be lost in the dominant narrative of the area as deficient and corrupt. The problem with this single narrative of Jane and Finch is that it is one narrative of one community. Jane and Finch, in my experience, has never been one community with one type of people, with one story. This reminds me of the quote: "Until the lion learns to speak, the tales of hunting will always favour the hunter." In this regard, I am appreciative of the opportunity to share part of my story. Yet, just like the trepidation I felt in Grade 7, I also now wonder what this story will do. Will it disrupt or support the prevailing view that growing up in Jane and Finch was not a positive experience?

I think of being praised by my professors now and by my teachers in the past for my aspirations and the heights to which I have ascended. I am appreciative and humbled by their praise and support. But I wonder if, within the deficit thinking about Jane and Finch, these admirers are seeing me as "an example" of what this troubled community can produce. It is difficult to say for sure how preconceived ideas work to dominate our thought patterns when we are given a single representation of a community. Whatever the case, let me say here that anything I have done has never been in spite of or despite my community and upbringing. It is solely and unequivocally because of it. The social and political capital that I have gained through the learning afforded me by having to constantly challenge the existing single story (negative as it is) has given me drive, dedication and purpose. And it has also given me the words to tell my own story.

• • •

Kulsoom's and Sam's reflections alert us to the fact that Jane and Finch is a community of neighbourhoods. Hence, reducing community members and, in particular, students' experiences to a single narrative would mean failing to give attention to the complex, interwoven intricacies and enduring factors of what it means to live and attend school in this or any marginalized community.

Community, Class and Schooling: Toward a Community-Centred Approach to Education

The experiences, aspirations and achievements of both Kulsoom and Sam, and, of course, many other youth, indicate the critical if not decisive role that their working-class neighbourhood plays in their lives. Their stories also point to how their lives in school are the product of their interactions with and influence of parents, peers, teachers and significant others, with parental influence tending, at times, to overshadow the others. But what is clear is that they do not take their neighbourhood for granted — they cannot afford to, for as they recognize, their opportunities in life are mediated by the stigmatized low-income neighbourhood in which they reside.

Sociologists tell us that there is a direct relationship between the class background of individuals and the neighbourhoods in which we live — middle-class people tend to live in neighbourhoods with big houses, manicured lawns and tree-lined streets, and working-class people tend to live in neighbourhoods with low- and highrise apartment buildings, townhouses and small houses. Much of this has to do with the economic means of families, in that the house and neighbourhood where they can afford to live is based on the money (including income) and opportunities to which they have access. And as sociologists also tell us, one's salary or income, occupation, profession and education are all interrelated and collectively constitute the socio-economic status or social class of the person. This status is also mediated by factors such as ethnicity, race, gender, age, immigrant status (or years in the society) and language (e.g., fluency in the dominant language). Therefore, there is a direct relationship between the neighbourhood in which a person lives and his or her social class status. That some neighbourhoods are predominantly populated by a particular ethnic or racial group or by immigrants is just as significant as their economic means — that is, their social-class background.

The class position or the economic means of the people of a neighbourhood also helps to define the institutions such as schools, recreational centres and social service agencies that operate within it. In fact, in the case of schools, a recent *Toronto Star* series (Rushowy, Winsa and Ferguson 2011; Winsa and Rushowy 2011) reported that there is a "great divide" in the funding to which schools in the Greater Toronto Area have access based on the income level of the neighbourhoods in which they are located. Specifically, findings indicate that both public and Catholic schools

> with the highest amount of school generated funds in 2008–09 are located in the city's affluent areas, while the bottom 20 were mostly in Toronto's poorer neighbourhoods. School-generated funds include fundraising by school parent councils as well as any fees collected by the school from activities such as book fairs or year books. (Winsa and Rushowy 2011: A6)

Located in one of Toronto's poorest neighbourhoods, schools in the Jane and Finch area are unlikely to have the funding base that would enable them to obtain educational resources in addition to those provided by the school board. In other words, compared to their peers attending schools in higher income neighbourhoods, students in Jane and Finch schools are at an educational disadvantage because of the lack of economic resources generated by the informal parent-driven fundraising activities (Frenette 2007).

But irrespective of the class position of neighbourhoods or the economic means of parents, the principles, norms and values by which institutions — in this case, schools — operate are dominated by the middle-class Eurocentric ethos of the society.[1] Operating with such an ethos, schools are unlikely to effectively serve members in working-class or low-income neighbourhoods because of the differences in the culture of the schools from that of the neighbourhoods. This difference between the school and community is maintained through parents' and community members' lack of both economic resources and the social, cultural and political capital necessary to insist on, influence and/or ensure appropriate culturally relevant and responsive schooling and education for their children. The idea of schooling in low-income, disadvantaged neighbourhoods should not be merely about preparing students to "get out" of the neighbourhood. Nor should it be about students serving as models for their peers or the imperative to passively accept the notion that, through schooling, combined with their hard work, resilience and perseverance, they will realize their occupational ambitions despite the powerfully coercive effects of poverty, classism, racism, sexism and xenophobia. Individual actions that fail to recognize the structural factors that operate as barriers to achievement will not produce the necessary school reforms. What is needed, therefore, is a collaboration and partnership between youth, parents, community members and educators "with a clear mission to do whatever is necessary to improve the quality of education for all students in the system" (Renée and McAlister 2011: 2). Indeed, a strong school-community relationship has the "potential to advance equity [and] create innovative solutions that reflect the interests and experiences of disenfranchised communities" and, in the process, build the needed social capital of these communities and schools (9).

There is no doubt that strong school-community relationships exist in White middle- and upper-class communities where the principles, values and norms of the schools are reflective of those of the community. As such, it is fair to say that in these communities a community-referenced approach to education is already in place. The same approach is needed for students in marginalized communities if they are to engage with and benefit from their schooling in the way that their middle- and upper-class peers do. A community-referenced approach to education ensures that the lessons, curriculum,[2] pedagogy and resources help students to make sense of their community and their own social situation. Hence, educators must have knowledge of the community[3] and the culture[4] if they are to effectively facilitate a teaching and learning process in which students are able to see the relevance of their learning to their lives. Cammarota (2008: 135) writes that when "students witness the validation of their culture within the educational process, they concatenate their identities as family members and students." And most importantly, as the "cultural substance of their identities feeds and sustains an academic persona," and teachers acknowledge the "valid and sophisticated knowledge" that is contained within students' culture, students are able to "see themselves as knowledgeable." As such, the curriculum must be inclusive of the diverse experiences of the students, thereby making learning community-based and culturally relevant and responsive to them. Cammarota goes on to say,

> Allowing students to participate in constructing the learning process encourages them to perceive education as their project, something they create. Tapping into the creative spirit of young people will render education exciting and thus inspire them to learn. They no longer feel that education is something being done to them by somebody else, but something they are doing to recreate themselves and their lived contexts. (137)

In *Revolutionizing Education: Youth Participatory Action Research in Motion*, Cammarota and Fine (2008), their colleagues and students report on what can be accomplished by students and teachers when education is done differently: when "students learn how to use culture as 'Funds of Knowledge' to generate more equitable social relations to ameliorate conditions and opportunities for themselves, families and communities" (136). With a social justice framework, students come to understand and act upon the societal roots and causes of the social conditions and the problems they encounter in their daily lives. They also learn to make the connection between oppression as related to classism, racism, sexism and homophobia, and antisocial or maladaptive behaviours (e.g., criminal behaviour, violent tendencies and substance addiction), thus removing "any doubts in the student's mind that she or he is to blame for her or his struggles" (138). The pedagogy used in the education of students is participatory action research (PAR), by which students, with key research questions, conduct research using methods such as "participant observations, qualitative interviews and questionnaires, films and speak out" (5). Ginwright (2008: 21) maintains that through this "emancipatory research" young people are able to "develop skills both to explain systemic causes of issues that shape their lives and to act to transform these conditions."

The PAR approach to learning based on a social justice framework has proved quite invaluable to students. Kim Dominguez, one of the students who grew up, as she put it, "on food stamps, welfare, and attended low income schools" writes in her essay "Voice of the Voiceless: 'Because We Are All So Silenced'" that "my class of about 15 students who were disenfranchised by our school system and labeled as 'at risk,' were given the opportunity not only to speak out in class and talk about our personal struggles and how they affect our education but also to create a documentary based on the research we conducted in class through filming, interviews, field notes, photography, and poetry" (in Cammarota and Fine 2008: 140). She credits her participation in a learning process in which she investigated her social world and followed her curiosity for her accomplishments — the chance to meet a "Chicano Congressman in Washington, and to travel to Montreal, Canada, to present at an education conference." Another student, Luis Valdez, also credits this approach to his education for the fact that he will not be going through life "as a halfway conscious, media-controlled drone," which would have been the case without the knowledge that he now has about social justice and what he has come to learn about the "injustices that were right under my nose and went through every day. I once heard someone say," Valdez continues, "that a penguin does not know how cold the water he is swimming in is until he knows of the warmth of tropical waters" (141).

Do teachers have to be from the community or neighbourhood, or of the same race, ethnic and class backgrounds as the students to facilitate a culturally relevant and responsive learning and teaching process? While a case can be made about the usefulness and expediency of teachers and students having shared experiences, ultimately, as has been repeatedly demonstrated with students such as Dominguez and Valdez (see also Kendra and Conrad in Chapter 4), it is those teachers who encourage students to be active participants in their learning, as opposed to passive recipients of information, who will make the educational process meaningful and productive for students. Such teachers engage students in a teaching and learning process that recognizes the community as a source of cultural and social capital or "cultural wealth" (see Yosso 2005). They encourage them to use their sociological lens in assignments to construct narratives of their communities from their explorations or observations of people's movements, interactions and other activities. Further, informed by an equity and social justice framework, such teachers work to have schools and classrooms where there is a free exchange of ideas, tools and "democratization of knowledge" (Ginwright 2008: 21) that contributes to collective knowledge-making, thereby opening up opportunities and possibilities for students.

It is certainly important to encourage young people to have hope, hold onto high aspirations and believe that through their agency they can succeed in life. But encouraging a perception of their community as a place from which to escape could impair some young people's understandings of schooling. They could come to see school as the place where they go to confirm the pathologies of their neighbourhood life and not the complicity of the society in these pathologies. From this perspective, young people are likely to view their community, like many other people, including their teachers, through a deficit lens. This lens also maintains that their own lives and the improvement of the community hinges exclusively on their own efforts and those of community members. Young people who buy into this individualized view of their ambitions will be marked as extra-ordinary, and others as lazy, apathetic and slackers — the ones who will eventually be classified as "at risk." Missing in this understanding are the ways in which the community operates as a "school," providing the edu-cation, the social and cultural capital and supports that not only help to motivate its young people for success, but the talent, skills and reasons to do so. Indeed, parents in low-income communities, and immigrant parents in particular, wish for their children to live under better circumstances than they do or did, and as such, they tend to rely (or bank) on education to make this a reality. Therefore, what we need are schools that facilitate students' acquisition of skills and credentials that will lead to social and economic advancement because of the emancipatory powers of education structured on meritocracy, egalitarianism and democracy.

Conclusion

We do not say that all students will receive "the same" education. Instead, we see multiple curricula, modified curricula, adapted curricula, differentiated education, differentiated programs, individual education plans (IEPs), and a host of similar accom-modations to meet individual student needs. Educators are agreed that equity in educational programming does not mean all students should receive the same educational programming. (Reimer 2005: 4)

Clearly, if schools in urban and suburban disadvantaged neighbourhoods are to effectively meet the needs of their students, then they must develop educational programs, curricula and pedagogy that reference the commu-nity. This community-referenced approach begins with an understanding that the students' lives — their experiences, needs, interests, expectations and aspirations — are mediated by the communities in which they live. Of course, students' lives are first and foremost shaped by their parents and family members, but in the absence of information about families, a reasonable starting point to knowing the students is getting to know the community. This is not to say, as demonstrated by Kulsoom and Sam, that everyone who lives in a community is going to be the same or have the same relationship to the community. But whatever their particular needs and expectations are of their schooling, the community — in terms of how both insiders and outsiders construct it — plays a significant role in students' sense of self and perception of their possibilities in life. Understandably, it might be easier to get to know the community with all its complexity and diversity than the family culture or the circumstances of each student. And while family composition, race, ethnicity, religion, language, citizenship and immigrant status might provide some insights into the familial culture of students, that culture is also mediated by that of the community in which they live and the imagined geographic and social boundaries that they construct for themselves or others construct for them.[5] Teachers' knowledge of the community and their students is fundamental to building a relationship with them that is an essential component of effective teaching. That relationship requires educators to acknowledge the cultural selves as well as the readings and perceptions of students and the community that they bring to their teaching. In other words, teachers need to acknowledge that the "knapsack" (McIntosh 1988) of information and privileges they bring to their interactions with students contributes to the exchange relationship that is teaching. With this knowledge, therefore, it is our task as educators to locate ourselves in our relationships with students and create educational experiences that centre and validate their cultural, familial and community life.

Notes

1.   It is likely to be different with grassroots organizations or schools that are established and run by community members.

2.   I take curriculum to be more than documents that set out an educational program, course content and materials. What is communicated through curriculum is influenced by who decides and develops the curriculum as well as the people that the curriculum designers imagine the students to be. So, curriculum is not a static document or neutral text, but a complex, dynamic, theoretically informed text and/or instrument that includes pedagogical engagement of participants (or students) in relation to their lived experiences. As such, curriculum should be developed through dialogue.

3.   I wish to emphasize that community is more than geography. From a sociological perspective, communities are constructs and are not solely determined by those assumed to be living within them or identified as belonging to them. Significantly, communities are never singular or "stand-alone" but are often nestled within larger communities. The norms, values, practices and interests and beliefs of any community — the "culture" of a community — are, importantly, learned and shared among its members.

4.   Conceptually speaking, culture, simply put, refers to the way in which people in a society, community or group organize and conduct themselves. It consists of a dynamic and complex set of values, beliefs, norms, patterns of thinking, styles of communication, linguistic expressions and ways of interpreting and interacting with the world that assist individuals in making sense of their existence and live through their varied circumstances. Individuals are not only influenced or shaped by the culture of their group, community and society, but also shape it (James 2010b).

5.   Middle-class youth or those in other "unbounded" communities imagine more expansive space and a wider range of options and entitlement.

References

Anisef, P., P. Axelrod, E. Baichman, C.E. James and T. Turrittin. 2000. *Opportunity and Uncertainty: Life Course Experiences of the Class of '73.* Toronto: University of Toronto Press.

Ballantyne, R. 2007. "Jully Black Is Back." *Popjournalism.* February 10. At <robertbal-lantyne.com/2006/09/18/jully-black-is-back/>.

Barber, J. 1999. "Can Anything Good Come Out of This Place?" *Globe and Mail*, June 29, p. A1.

Bashi, V. 2004. "Globalized Anti-Blackness: Transnationalizing Western Immigration Law, Policy, and Practice." *Ethnic and Racial Studies* 27, 4: 584–606.

Begin, M., and G.L. Caplan. 1994. *For the Love of Learning.* Toronto: Ontario Royal Commission on Learning. At <edu.gov.on.ca/eng/general/abcs/rcom/full/>.

Benjamin, C. 2010. "Rebuilding Halifax's Most Feared Neighbourhood, One Project at a Time." *Globe and Mail*, September 24. At <chrisbenjaminwriting.com/rebuilding-halifaxs-most-feared-neighbourhood.php>.

Berry, L.M. 2000. "Corridor of Power: Community Organizers Turn Negative Perceptions into Positive Results in the Troubled Jane-Finch Area." *EYE Toronto*, September 7.

Bhattacharjee, K. 2003. *The Ontario Safe Schools Act: School Discipline and Discrimination.* Toronto: Ontario Human Rights Commission.

Boesveld, S. 2010. "All-Boys Schools Foster 'Achievement Culture.'" *Globe and Mail*, September 17. At <theglobeandmail.com/life/family-and-relationships/all-boys-schools-foster-achievement-culture/article1332995/>.

Bourke, A., and A.J. Jayman. 2010. "Between Vulnerability and Risk: Promoting Access and Equity in a School-University Partnership Program." *Urban Education* 46, 1: 76–98.

Brantlinger, E. 2003. "Who Wins and Who Loses? Social Class and Student Identities." In M. Sadowski (ed.), *Adolescents at School: Perspectives on Youth, Identity, and Education.* Cambridge, MA: Harvard Education Press.

Brathwaite, K.S., and C.E. James (eds.). 1996. *Educating African Canadians.* Toronto: James Lorimer & Company.

Brown, K., V. Kennedy, and M. Shin. 2005. "Students Live in Fear." *Toronto Star*, September 14, p. A23.

Brown, L. 2011a. "Monitoring Becomes Mentoring; Streetwise Guides Reach Out to Help Young Wayward Students." *Toronto Star*, January 28. At <thestar.com/article/930009--school-safety-monitors-more-mentor-than-muscle>.

___. 2011b. "Plan for Africentic High School Put on Hold Amid Packed and Angry Protest." *Toronto Star*, March 30. At <thestar.com/printarticle/965530>.

Caldwell, C. 2005. "Revolting High Rises." *New York Times Magazine*, November 27. At <nytimes.com/2005/11/27/magazine/27wwln_essay.html>.

Cammarota, J. 2008. "Participatory Action Research in the Public School Curriculum: Toward a Pedagogy of Dialogical Authoring." In J. Cammarota and M. Fine (eds.), *Revolutionizing Education: Youth Participatory Action Research in Motion* (pp.

135–138). New York: Routledge.

Cammarota, J., and M. Fine (eds.). 2008. *Revolutionizing Education: Youth Participatory Action Research in Motion.* New York: Routledge.

Campbell, M. 2007. "Toronto FC Selection Living a Sweet Dream." *Toronto Star*, January 19. At <thestar.com/Sports/article/172735>.

Carniol, N., and I. Teotonio. 2005. "Seized Gun Linked to Shootout." *Toronto Star*, December 30, p. A01.

CBC (Canadian Broadcasting Corporation). 2007. Toronto. "Lost in the Struggle." *The Fifth Estate.* Originally aired October 4, 2006.

___. 2007. Toronto. "Growing Up Without Men." *Metro Morning.* At <cbc.ca/toronto/features/withoutmen.html>. Retrieved January 2011.

Christoff, S., and S. Kalache. 2007. "The Poorest Postal Code." *The Dominion* 42. At <dominionpaper.ca/articles/909>.

City of Calgary. 2010. "Community Social Statistics: Forest Lawn." City of Calgary Civic Census 2009. Community and Neighbourhood Services, Social Policy and Planning Division. At <calgary.ca/CSPS/CNS/Documents/community_social_statistics/forest_lawn.pdf>.

City of Toronto. 2008. *Jane-Finch: Priority Area Profile.* Prepared by the Social Policy Analysis & Research Section in the Social Development, Finance and Administration Division Source: Census 2006. At <toronto.ca/demographics/pdf/priority2006/area_janefinch_full.pdf>.

College Student Alliance (CSA), OSTA-AECO, and OUSA. 2011. *Breaking Barriers: A Strategy for Equal Access to Higher Education.* February. At <ousa.ca/wordpress/wp-content/uploads/.../Breaking-Barriers.pdf>.

Contenta, S. 1993. *Rituals of Failure: What Schools Really Teach.* Toronto: Between the Lines.

CTV Toronto. 2007. "Suspect in T.O. School Shooting Still at Large." May 23. At <ctv.ca/CTVNews/CTVNewsAt11/20070523/school_shooting_070523/>.

Cummins, J. 2001. "From Multicultural to Anti-Racist Education: An Analysis of Programmes and Policies in Ontario." In C. Baker and N.H. Hornberger (eds.), *An Introductory Reader to the Writings of Jim Cummins.* UK: Multilingual Matters.

Dale, D. 2010. "Toronto Policed by Out-of-towners." *Toronto Star*, September 3. At <www.thestar.com/news/gta/article/856817--toronto-policed-by-out-of-towners>.

Daloz, L.A., C. Keen, J. Keen and S.D. Parks. 1996. *Common Fire: Leading Lives of Commitment in a Complex World.* Boston: Beacon Press.

Daniel, Y., and K. Bondy. 2008. "Safe Schools and Zero Tolerance: Policy, Program and Practice in Ontario." *Canadian Journal of Educational Administration and Policy* 70. At <umanitoba.ca/publications/cjeap/currentissues.html>.

Dei, G.S., I.M. James, L.L. Karumanchery, S. James-Wilson, and J. Zine. 2000. *Removing the Margins: The Challenges and Possibilities of Inclusive Schooling.* Toronto: Canadian Scholars' Press.

Diebel, L. 2007. "'Where Are the Men?' There's a Hidden Crisis in This City." *Toronto Star*, August 19, p. A1.

Deverteuil, G., and K. Wilson. 2010. "Reconciling Indigenous Need with the Urban Welfare State: Evidence of Culturally-Appropriate Services and Spaces for Aboriginals in Winnipeg, Canada." *Geoforum* 41, 3: 498–507.

DiManno. 2005. "We're Now Paying Steep Price for Nihilism; City Takes Another Kick in the Gut." *Toronto Star*, December 28, p. AO6.

References

___. 2007a. "'Don't Die, Jordan,' Best Friend Pleaded." *Toronto Star,* May 25. At <thestar. com/News/article/217619>.

___. 2007b. "A Heartbreaking Sendoff for the 'Prince of Shoreham.'" *Toronto Star,* June 1. At <thestar.com/article/220221>.

___. 2010. "Race Not an Issue in Jordan Manners Trial." *Toronto Star,* February 5. At <thestar.com/news/gta/article/760928>.

Dippo, D., and C. James. 2011. "The Urbanization of Suburbia: Implications for Inner-Suburban Schools and Communities." In R. Keil, P. Wood, and D. Young (eds.), *In-Between Infrastructure: Urban Connectivity in an Age of Vulnerability.* Kelowna: UBC Praxis (e)Press.

Doucet, M. 1999. "Toronto in Transition: Demographic Change in the Late Twentieth Century." Toronto: CERIS–The Ontario Metropolis Centre, p. 19.

Douglas, P. 2007. "Mayor, Policy Chief Address Ongoing False Rumours." *Brampton Guardian,* August 5, p. 3.

Dowd, N.E. 1997. *In Defense of Single Parent Families.* New York: New York Press.

Duffy, A. 2003. "Newcomers Losing Ground." Special Report (pp. 18–19). Toronto: Atkinson Charitable Foundation. At <atkinsonfoundation.ca/files/Duffyrev.pdf>.

Ericson, R.V., and K.D. Haggerty. 1999. "Governing the Young." In R. Smandych (ed.), *Governable Places: Readings on Governmentality and Crime Control* (pp. 163–190). Hampshire: Ashgate Publishing.

Falconer, J., P. Edwards and L. MacKinnon. 2008. *The Road to Health: A Final Report on School Safety.* Report of the School Community Safety Panel. Toronto: Toronto District School Board.

Farmer, S. 2010. "Criminality of Black Youth in Inner-City Schools: 'Moral Panic,' Moral Imagination, and Moral Formation." *Race, Ethnicity and Education* 13, 3: 367–381.

Fawcett, G., and K. Scott. 2007. *A Lost Decade: Urban Poverty in Canada, 1990 to 2000.* Ottawa: Canadian Council on Social Development.

Fleras, A. 1995. "Please Adjust Your Set: Media and Minorities in a Multicultural Society." In B.D. Singer (ed.), *Communications in Canadian Society* (pp. 406–431). Toronto: Nelson Canada.

Fraser, N. 2011. "Guilt Trippin' and the Mothering of Black Boys in Toronto." Unpublished doctoral dissertation, Faculty of Graduate Studies, Education, York University, Toronto.

Freire, P. 1994. *Pedagogy of Hope: Reliving Pedagogy of the Oppressed.* New York: Continuum.

Frenette, M. 2007. "Why Are Youth from Lower-Income Families Less Likely to Attend University? Evidence from Academic Abilities, Parental Influences, and Financial Constraints." Analytical Studies Branch Research Paper Series. Ottawa: Statistics Canada.

Friesen, J. 2005. "Despair and Frustration at Jane and Finch." *Globe and Mail,* November 11, p. A14.

___. 2006. "One Neighbourhood, Three Schools, and a World of Difference for Students." *Globe and Mail,* June 23, p. A1.

Ginwright, S.A. 2007. "Black Youth Activism and the Role of Critical Social Capital in Black Community Organizations." *American Behavioral Scientist* 51, 3: 367–379.

___. 2008. "Collective Radical Imagination: Youth Participatory Action Research and the Art of Emancipatory Knowledge." In J. Cammarota and M. Fine (eds.), *Revolutionizing Education: Youth Participatory Action Research in Motion* (pp. 13–22). New York: Routledge.

Goddard, J. 2007. "Alwyn Barry, 18: Filmmaker 'Broke the Stereotype' on Jane-Finch." *Toronto Star*, December 15, p. A6.

Gosine, K., and C.E. James. 2010. "Racialized Students Resisting: Hindrance or Asset to Academic Success?" In B.J. Porfilio and P.R. Carr (eds.), *Youth Culture, Education and Resistance* (pp. 41–56). Rotterdam: Sense Publishers.

Graff, J. 2005. "Streets of Fire." *Time*, Europe Edition, November 6. At <time.com/time/magazine/article/0,9171,1126690,00.html>.

Grant, C.A., and A. Portera (eds.). 2011. "Intercultural and Multicultural Education: Enhancing Global Interconnectedness." London, New York: Routledge.

Gray, J. 2005. "Miller Meets with Creba Family." *Globe and Mail*, December 30, p. A7.

Hall, T.H. 2008. "Brand Jane-Finch: A Critical Discourse Analysis of Print Media Discourse on a Toronto Low Income Community." Unpublished master's thesis, Graduate Program in Communication and Culture, York University, Toronto.

Han Nguyen, A. 2005. "The Controversial Music Video from Chuckie Akenz." *Viet Weekly*, March 31. At <jane-finch.com/articles/yougotbeef.htm>.

Hann, M. 2005. "The Decline of the Immigrant Home-Ownership Advantage: Life-cycle, Declining Fortunes and Changing Housing Careers in Montreal, Toronto and Vancouver, 1981–2001." *Urban Studies* 42, 12: 2191–2212.

Henry, F., and C. Tator. 2006. *The Colour of Democracy: Racism in Canadian Society*. Toronto: ITP Nelson.

Henze, R.C. 2005. "Veronica's Story: Reflections on the Limitations of Support Systems." In L. Pease-Alvarez and S. Schecter (eds.), *Learning, Teaching and Community: Contributions of Situated and Participatory Approaches to Educational Innovation* (pp. 257–276). Mahwah, NJ: Lawrence Erlbaum.

Hidalgo, N.M. 1997. "A Layering of Family and Friends: Four Puerto Rican Families' Meaning of Community." *Education and Urban Society* 30, 1: 20–40.

Higgins, D. 2001. "CBC Race Ruckus: Documentary on Street Rappers Infuriates Jane-Finch Community." *Now Magazine*, August 30, p. 1.

Ippolito, J., and S.R. Schecter. 2008. "A School-Based Research Approach for Responding to the Literacy Needs of Linguistically Diverse Families." *Education Canada* 48, 2: 55–58.

James, C.E. 1997. "Contradictory Tensions in the Experiences of African Canadians in a Faculty of Education with an Access Program." *Canadian Journal of Education* 22, 2: 158–174.

___. 2000. "'You're Doing It for the Students': On the Question of Role Models." In C.E. James (ed.), *Experiencing Difference* (pp. 89–89). Halifax: Fernwood Publishing.

___. 2005. "Constructing Aspirations: The Significance of Community in the Schooling Lives of Children of Immigrants." In L. Pease-Alvarez and S.R. Schecter (eds.), *Learning, Teaching, and Community: Contributions of Situated and Participatory Approaches to Educational Innovation* (pp. 217–233). New Jersey: Lawrence Erlbaum Associates.

___. 2008. "'Armed and Dangerous'/'Known to Police': Racializing Suspects." In B. Schissel and C. Brooks (eds.), *Marginality and Condemnation: An Introduction to Criminology* (pp. 378–403). Halifax: Fernwood Publishing.

___. 2009. "Masculinity, Racialization, and Schooling: The Making of Marginalized Men." In W. Martino, M. Kehler, and M.B. Weaver-Hightower (eds.), *The Problem with Boys' Education: Beyond the Backlash* (pp. 102–123). New York: Routledge.

___. 2010a. *Seeing Ourselves: Exploring Race, Ethnicity and Culture*. Toronto: Thompson Educational Publishing.

___. 2010b. "Schooling and the University Plans of Immigrant Black Students From an Urban Neighbourhood." In R. Milner (ed.), *Culture, Curriculum, and Identity in Education* (pp. 117–139). New York: Palgrave Macmillan.

___. 2011. "Multicultural Education in a Color-Blind Society." In C.A. Grant and A. Portera (eds.), *Intercultural and Multicultural Education: Enhancing GlobalConnectedness* (pp. 191–210). New York: Routledge.

___. 2012. "Troubling Role Models: Seeing Racialization in the Discourse Relating to 'Corrective Agents' for Black Males." In K. Moffat (ed.), *Troubled Masculinties: Re-Imagining Urban Men* (pp. 77–92). Toronto: University of Toronto Press.

James, C.E., and C. Haig-Brown. 2001. "'Returning the Dues': Community and the Personal in a University–School Partnership." *Urban Education* 36, 2: 226–255.

James C.E., and L. Taylor. 2008. "'Education Will Get You to the Station:' Marginalized Students' Experience and Perceptions of Merit in Accessing University." *Canadian Journal of Education* 31, 3: 567–590.

___. 2010. "The Making of At Risk Students: How Youth See Teachers Thwarting Their Education." In C.C. Smith (ed.), *Anti-Racism in Education: Missing in Action* (pp. 123–136). Ottawa: Canadian Centre for Policy Alternatives.

Jane-Finch.com. 2008. "Police in Westview Consultation" [Video]. November 24. At <youtube.com/watch?v=781Ussn6NXI&feature=related>.

___. 2009. "Cops in Schools" [Video]. September 5. At <youtube.com/watch?v=e5VpagJPZWo>.

Krueger, P. 2010. "It's Not Just a Method! The Epistemic and Political Work of Young People's Lifeworlds at the School-Prison Nexus." *Race, Ethnicity and Education* 13, 3: 383–408.

Li, P. 2003. "The Place of Immigrants: The Politics of Difference in Territorial and Social Space." *Canadian Ethnic Studies* 2: 1–13.

López, N. 2002. "Race-Gender Experiences and Schooling: Second-Generation Dominican, West Indian, and Haitian Youth in New York City." *Race, Ethnicity and Education* 5, 1: 67–89.

MacNevin, W. 1999. *From the Edge: A Woman's Evolution from Abuse to Activism.* Toronto: Picas and Points Publishing.

MacQueen, K. 2008. "The Rankings: Canada's Most Dangerous Cities." *Maclean's*, March 5. At <2.macleans.ca/2010/10/14/national-crime-rankings-2010/>.

Mandell, N., and R. Sweet. 2004. "Parental Involvement in the Creation of Home Learning Environments: Gender and Class Patterns." In R. Sweet and P. Anisef (eds.), *Preparing for Post-Secondary Education: New Roles for Governments and Families.* Montreal: McGill-Queen's University Press.

Marlow, I. 2007. "'Busted' School System Failed Jordan Manners, Teacher Says; Officials in Denial Played Down Violence, Says Special-Ed Chief Who Saw Warning Signs." *Toronto Star*, June 2. At < thestar.com/News/article/220731>.

Marlow, I., and B. Powell. 2007. "Police Raid Nothing New for Some." *Toronto Star*, June 16. At <thestar.com/News/article/226116>.

Martino, W., and G. Rezai-Rashti. 2010. "Male Teacher Shortage: Black Teachers' Perspectives." *Gender and Education* 22, 3: 247–262.

McCready, L.T. 2010. *Making Space for Diverse Masculinities: Difference, Intersectionality, and Engagement in an Urban High School.* New York: Peter Lang Publishing.

McGahan, P. 1995. *Urban Sociology in Canada.* Toronto: Harcourt Brace and Co.

McIntosh, P. 1988. "White Privilege and Male Privilege: A Personal Account of Coming to See Correspondence Through Work in Women's Studies." In M.L. Andersen and P. Hill Collins (eds.), *Race Class and Gender: An Anthology* (pp. 70–81). Belmont, CA: Wadsworth.

McKell, L. 2010. "Achievement Gap Task Force: Draft Report." Toronto: Toronto District School Board.

McLaren, P. 1981. *Cries from the Corridor: The New Suburban Ghettos*. Toronto: Methuen.

___. 1988. *Life in Schools: An Introduction to Critical Pedagogy in the Foundations of Education*. White Plains, NY: Longman.

McMurty, R., and A. Curling. 2008. *Review of the Roots of Youth Violence*, Vol. 1. Toronto: Government of Ontario.

Meiners, E.R., and M.T. Winn. 2010. "Resisting the School to Prison Pipeline: The Practice to Build Abolition Democracies." *Race, Ethnicity and Education* 13, 3: 271–276.

Mensah, J. 2010. *Black Canadians: History, Experience, Social Conditions*. Halifax: Fernwood Publishing.

Milan, A., and Tran, K. (2004). "Blacks in Canada: A Long History." *Canadian Social Trends* (Spring). Cat. no. 11-008. Ottawa: Statistics Canada.

Milner, H.R. 2006. "Pre-service Teachers' Learning about Cultural and Racial Diversity Implications for Urban Education." *Urban Education* 41, 4: 343–375.

Morgan, M. 2005. "I Wish My Friends Were White Girls." *Mellow Mood: The End of the Beginning*. Independent CD.

Murdie, R.A., and S. Ghosh. 2010. "Does Spatial Concentration Always Mean a Lack of Integration? Exploring Ethnic Concentration and Integration in Toronto." *Journal of Ethnic and Migration Studies* 36, 2: 293–311.

Murdie, R., and C. Teixeira. 2000. "Towards a Comfortable Neighbourhood and Appropriate Housing: Immigrant Experience in Toronto." Working Paper No. 10. Toronto: CERIS–The Ontario Metropolis Centre.

Myles, J., and F. Hou. 2004. "Changing Colours: Spatial Assimilation and New Racial Minority Immigrants." *Canadian Journal of Sociology* 29, 1: 29–58.

O'Grady, W., P.F. Parnaby, and J. Schikschneit,. 2010. "Guns, Gangs, and the Underclass: A Constructionist Analysis of Gun Violence in a Toronto High School." *Canadian Journal of Criminology and Criminal Justice* 52: 55–77.

Odih, P. 2002. "Mentors and Role Models: Masculinity and the Educational 'Underachievement' of Young Afro-Caribbean Males." *Race, Ethnicity and Education* 5, 1: 91–105.

O'Toole, M. 2011. "Jury Finds Defendants Not Guilty in Manners Retrial." *National Post*, May 19. At <news.nationalpost.com/2011/05/19/jury-finds-defendants-not-guilty-in-manners-retrial/>.

Pacini-Ketchabaw, V., and S. Schecter. 2002. "Engaging the Discourse of Diversity: Educators' Frameworks for Working with Linguistic and Cultural Difference." *Contemporary Issues in Early Childhood* 3, 3: 400–414.

Patriakou, E.N., R.P. Weisberg, S. Redding, and H.J. Walberg. 2005. *School–Family Partnerships for Children's Success*. New York: Teacher's College Press.

Powell, B. 2010. *Bad Seeds: The True Story of Toronto's Galloway Boys Street Gang*. Etobicoke, ON: John Wiley and Sons.

Rankin, J. 2010. "Carded: Probing a Racial Disparity." *Toronto Star*, February 6, p. A1.

Reimer, A. 2005. "Equity in Public Education." *Manitoba Association of School Superintendents* 2, 1. At <mass.mb.ca/EquityinPublic_Educ.pdf>.

Reinhart, A. 2005. "He Could Live Anywhere, but Jane-Finch is Home." *Globe and Mail*, December 13, p. A1.

Renée, M., and S. McAlister. 2011. *The Strengths and Challenges of Community Organizing as an Education Reform Strategy: What the Research Says; Executive Summary*. Prepared by the Annenberg Institute for School Reform at Brown University. Quincy, MA: Nellie Mae Education Foundation.

Rezai-Rashti, G., and W. Martino. 2010. "Black Male Teachers as Role Models: Resisting the Homogenizing Impulse of Gender and Racial Affiliation." *American Educational Research Journal* 47, 1: 37–64.

Richardson, C. 2008. "'Canada's Toughest Neighbourhood': Surveillance, Myth and Orientalism in Jane-Finch." Unpublished master's thesis, Faculty of Social Sciences, Brock University, St. Catharines, ON.

Risling, R., and S. Simmie. 2008. "What Is Poverty to a Kid?" [Video]. *Toronto Star*, April 17. At <thestar.com/news/article/416081>.

Rivers, E. 2005. "The Sins of the Father Are Visited on Black Youth." *Globe and Mail*, December 2, p. A23.

Rushowy, K. 2007. "Black-Focused School Debate Set." *Toronto Star*, November 7. At <thestar.com/News/Ontario/article/274299>.

Rushowy, K., P. Winsa, and B. Ferguson. 2011. "Province Needs to Set Fundraising Limits, Groups Say." *Toronto Star*, March 1. At <thestar.com/mobile/NEWS/article/946344>.

Ruttan, S. 2007. "From No. 1 to No. 213 in Local Quality of Life." *Edmonton Journal*, May 13. At <canada.com/edmontonjournal/story.html?id=ddcc7a67-505b-4ba5-baa1-5bb9b8adc7f0&k=1987>.

Sakamoto, J. 1986. "How Jane-Finch Was Born." *Toronto Star*, November 30, p. F01.

San Vicente, R.M. 2011. "Learning Through Mentorship: Accessing Opportunities to Support Boys." Toronto: York Centre for Education and Community. At <yorku.ca/ycec/?page_id=366>.

Schecter, S.R., and R. Bailey. 2002. *Language as Cultural Practice: Mexicanos en el norte*. Mahwah, NJ: Laurence Erlbaum Associates.

Sevier, B., and C. Ashcraft. 2007. "Be Careful What You Ask For: Exploring the Confusion Around the Usefulness of the Male Teacher as Male Role Model Discourse." *Men and Masculinities* 20, 10: 1–35.

Sheppard, M. 1997. "Jane-Finch's Bad Reputation Isn't Justified." *Toronto Star*, September 22, p. B3.

Silver, J. 2008. "Public Housing Risks and Alternatives: Uniacke Square in North End Halifax." Winnipeg: Canadian Centre for Policy Alternatives.

Southworth, N. 2000. "Jane-Finch Slaying Caught on Videotape." *Globe and Mail*, July 26, p. A18.

Srikanthan, T. 2007. "Chevon Was a Sweet, 'Strong-Willed' Boy." *Toronto Star*, June 10. At <thestar.com/News/article/223703>.

Star Phoenix [Saskatoon]. 2007. "Canadian Soccer Skills Need Polish." August 7. At <canada.com/saskatoonstarphoenix/news/sports/story.html?id=e00f234b-3b07-4dd1-ae68-d7e16af6cbc8>.

Statistics Canada. (2006). *Report of the Pan-Canadian Education Indicators Program*. Catalogue no. 81-582-XIE. Ottawa: Statistics Canada.

Sway. 2011. "Community Spotlight: Jane and Finch." Summer, pp. 36–42.

Toronto District School Board. 2000. "Equity Foundation Statement & Commitments to Equity Policy Implementation." At <tdsb.on.ca/_site/viewitem.asp?siteid=15

&menuid=682&pageid=546>.

Toronto Star. 2008. "Reject Black-Focused School: McGuinty." February 1. At <thestar. com/article/299431>.

Towards a New Beginning. 1992. The Report and Action Plan of the Four-level Government/African Canadian Community Working Group. Toronto: City of Toronto.

Vaccaro, M. 2011. "Oakwood Collegiate Proposed as T.O.'s Africentic High School But Nobody Asked the Students First." *Toronto Life,* March 28. At <torontolife.com/ daily/informer/the-new-normal/2011/03/28/oakwood-collegiate-proposed-as-t-o-%E2%80%99s-first-africentric-high-school%E2%80%94but-nobody-asked-the-students-first/>.

van Dijk, T.A. 2000. "New(s) Racism: A Discourse Analytical Approach." In S. Cottle (ed.), *Ethnic Minorities and the Media* (pp. 33–49). Philadelphia: Open University Press.

Wacquant, L. 2008. *Urban Outcasts: A Comparative Sociology of Advanced Marginality.* Cambridge, UK: Polity Press.

Wallace, A. 2009. "The Test: Africentric Schools Could Be the Key to Success for a Generation at Risk (Just Don't Call It Segregation)." *This Magazine,* January/ February, p. 4.

Wiens, M. 2005. "Jane and Finch." *Sounds Like Canada.* CBC Radio. Aired December 2, 2005.

Williams, C., and J. Clarke. 2003. "Toronto Community Profile." Racism, Violence and Health Project. Halifax: Dalhousie University.

Winsa, P., and K. Rushowy. 2011. "Rich Schools Get Richer as Private Cash Floods System." *Toronto Star,* February 28, p. A6.

Wood, J. 2011. "Schools Aim to Close Academic Gap among Aboriginal Students; First Nation, Metis Trail Non-Aboriginals in Grades, Graduation." *Star Phoenix* [Saskatoon], January 10, p. A1.

Wood, M. 2011. "Banking on Education: Black Canadian Females and Schooling." Unpublished doctoral dissertation, Faculty of Graduate Studies, Education, York University, Toronto.

Wortley, S. 2008. "Misrepresentation or Reality? The Depiction of Race and Crime in the Toronto Print Media." In B. Schissel and C. Brooks (eds.), *Marginality and Condemnation: An Introduction to Criminology* (pp. 104–134). Halifax: Fernwood Publishing.

Y-life. 2005. "PM 'Accessible' at Jane-Finch Stop, Says Poli Sci Student." November 14. At < yorku.ca/ylife/2005/11-14/index.htm>.

Yosso, T.J. 2005. "Whose Culture Has Capital? A Critical Race Theory Discussion of Community Cultural Wealth." *Ethnicity and Education* 8, 1: 69–91.